Craig Monson

Craig Monson

■ ■ ■

OG Bodybuilding Legend

Josh Bryant and Adam benShea

Craig Monson: OG Bodybuilding Legend

JoshStrength, LLC and Adam benShea

Copyright © 2021

Table of Contents

Foreword
by Danny Trejo

I first met Craig Monson in 1977. I'd just moved to Venice Beach, and I wandered into the weight pit (aka Muscle Beach) and started working out. Now, back then, you could get a whole lot of attitude just walking into the pit. There were a bunch of bodybuilders working out, and they can give off the vibe of "you're not welcome." And remember, I was a little guy compared to these monsters, just 160 pounds. Immediately, Craig Munson came over and said hello. He made me feel welcome.

Craig and I started cutting it up, talking, and I immediately knew who he was. I had been out of the Pen for a while, but I still knew people who knew people. Craig was known as "Tow Truck" inside, but had a solid reputation as a righteous dude.

One thing that Craig wasn't and hated, just like me, was bullies. He had a great spirit about him. He was so big and menacing, but his demeanor was immediately disarming. But no one would or could ever or in any way mistake his kindness for weakness. Craig is the kind of man who can terrify others with just a look.

Working out with Craig was incredible. Just moving all those plates on and off the bars with him was my workout. You have to remember that Craig was benching in the 500s, and that was just to push a lot of reps. Other bodybuilders almost didn't want to stand near him because he'd make them look small. But he wasn't vain, he was cool. He'd always work out with a shirt on and just get into it and do his thing.

I remember me and an old partner named Joe Mack went to a bodybuilding competition in Palm Springs where Craig was doing an exhibition. It was the first time I'd ever been to one, and I was just so blown away. I immediately realized what an art form it was. Even all the bodybuilders competing went wild when Craig posed. He got a standing ovation.

One time there was a bodybuilding competition at Venice Beach, and some guy was yapping and Craig got up and flexed, and thousands of people at the beach went wild. He had that effect on people. He's electrifying. Craig's greatest quality is his humility, and it takes a strong man to have humility. Craig, with his size and strength, could be the kind of guy who could charge people 50 cents just to walk around, but he makes people feel welcome.

Craig's story is so important and mirrors my own in the sense that his success tells people, especially young men from hard neighborhoods, if you get in trouble, that doesn't have to be the end of your story. You can make something of your life. Remember, it doesn't matter where you start, it's where you finish. I would watch the time, care, and attention he gave to young kids who looked up to him, and I was always impressed by that. He was generous with his time and expertise, perhaps the greatest gifts you can give another.

Craig is not only an incredible ambassador for bodybuilding, but for life in general. His story of redemption and purpose allows others to see it as a possibility. It gives them permission to live a different way. We are all granted one precious life, and what we do with our time is what counts. Instead of being a statistic of the streets, Craig became a legend.

Most importantly to me, he's always been a friend and has been since the first day I met him on the beach almost 50 years ago.

Danny Trejo
Los Angeles, CA
January 2021

Craig Monson with Danny Trejo at Venice Beach

Preface

This is a book about the life of Craig Monson. It is also a book about Craig Monson's training. The book is divided into four different sections.

The first part of the book covers Craig's early life, his childhood, his involvement with founding an infamous Los Angeles street gang, and his introduction to the iron.

The second segment tells of his time behind bars in some of the country's most notorious prisons.

The third portion recounts Big Monson's storied bodybuilding career.

The closing chapter shares Craig's life after he stepped away from the competitive stage.

At the closing of each section there is a training program that explains how Craig trained during that time of his life and how you can follow the same workout plan.

For a long time, Monson has been a man shrouded in mystery. It is now time to lift the veil of secrecy to reveal the life and training of Craig Monson.

Introduction

We are formed by our relationships. The walls we build and the scars we carry come from our relationships. Platonic, private, and public relationships make us who we are.

In the case of Craig Monson, his life was formed by his relationship with the iron. In a life with periods that dipped into the depths of deep valleys and rose to the pinnacles of high peaks, weight training was not just a constant in his life. The "pig iron" took "Big" Craig from the former to the latter—a strict adherence to training brought Craig out of his lowest points and up onto the bodybuilding stage to the acclaim of countless strength fans.

This is the story of a relationship, between a man and his passion, a human and his lifeline, Craig and his weights.

Chapter One

THE STORY

Every generation has their pivotal event. For Craig's generation, it was the assassination of John F. Kennedy. Where was he when he heard this seminal news? Unsurprisingly, lifting weights in his school gym.

But, before he found his way to the gym, Craig was born in a time and place rife with a level of persecution that would be hard for many in contemporary society to grasp.

One of 10 children, Craig Monson was born in Arkansas in 1950. His mother was that type of hardworking woman who would have been featured in many classic novels where the strong heroine bucks the odds and navigates around obstacles to make sure her children have a roof over their head, clothes on their back, and food on the table.

At that time, in that place, Craig's mother knew that her growing family needed to find greener pastures. Like any loving parent, she wanted her offspring to have a good life, one that was better than the one she knew in her childhood and perhaps even better than she could possibly imagine. So, like many black families in post–World War II America and like many families across time in the American story, they looked west. California, the land of the setting sun, offered a beacon of rising hope.

With her children, they boarded a Greyhound bus for their exodus from the scorching racism of the Deep South in the mid-20th century. The last sight of Arkansas was a reminder of just how horrific racial injustice was at that time. From the window of the Greyhound bus,

Craig's mother remembered seeing two black men hanging from a tree.

Southern California, with its palm trees, beaches, Mediterranean climate, and bright sunshine, seemed to be glowing with opportunity. However, as Craig would soon find out, Southern California, or Los Angeles, to be precise, was filled with its own unique challenges related to race, crime, and hardship. Of course, he would also eventually find a way to his spot in the sun.

Craig's formative years were spent in those areas of Los Angeles known as Watts and Compton, which would come to be glorified in the rap music scores of the early 1990s. Although Craig's childhood precedes much of the lyrical descriptions from the gangster rappers, his immediate influences were individuals and groups who would become the stuff of inner-city lore and notorious ghetto legends.

In the late 1950s and into the 1960s, there were a number of established gangs across south Los Angeles. Some of the more well-known gangs included the Businessmen, the Gladiators, and the Slauson Renegades. A number of individuals emerged from these gangs to gain recognition beyond urban strife and in the broader realm of social justice.

A dedicated member of the inner circle of the Slauson Renegades, Alprentice "Bunchy" Carter spent four years in Soledad prison for an armed robbery during the 1960s. While incarcerated, Carter was exposed to the doctrine of the Nation of Islam and the writings of Malcom X. However, after meeting Eldridge Cleaver (who was also incarcerated at Soledad), Bunchy broke away from the Nation of Islam. Carter's commitment to a secular expression of black liberation took shape when, upon his release from prison, he met the legendary Huey Newton. One of the founders of the Black Panther Party (BPP), Newton influenced Carter to join the party in 1967.

Bunchy's devotion to the BPP was evident with his move to start the Southern California chapter of the Black Panther Party. As a leader of the Black Panther Party in Los Angeles, Carter directed the group in its study of politics, poetry, and firearms. The party also provided social outreach programs, like a free breakfast for children. Carter, in particular, reached out to many in the community to serve as a powerful point of emulation.

Craig has fond memories of Bunchy Carter. A childhood friend to one of Bunchy's younger brothers, Craig remembers meeting and spending time with Carter after his release from prison. Bunchy would often come over to Craig's house to share his works of poetry. Bunchy's mentorship influenced Craig to join the Black Panther Party, which expanded Craig's worldview beyond his immediate surroundings of urban Los Angeles.

Other characters from the neighborhood would influence Craig in less political but perhaps more prominent ways.

Before handheld mobile devices became a seeming requirement for children and adults alike, kids in the 1950s and 1960s eagerly waited for their parents to take them to the movie theater. This was the highly anticipated entertainment of the time. With fondness, Craig remembers his mom taking him to see the actress Lana Turner on the big screen. With fondness, Craig also remembers seeing "Bird" from the Baby Slauson crew outside of the movie house.

In the vernacular of the time, Bird was "booted and suited." Decked out in a carefully chosen and pressed suit along with a fedora-style top hat, strategically tilted at a slight angle as if it was a nod of acknowledgment to the potential chaos lurking just under the surface of this immaculate dress, Bird would rise out from an old "Al Capone"–style car with "suicide doors" and all. On his arm, Bird had his beautiful Latina girlfriend.

This flashy display of style outside of the theater was as mesmerizing, influential, and impactful as anything Craig witnessed inside of the movie house. Craig processed the arrival of Bird in almost the same way that someone would take in a royal procession. With admiration and awe, Craig saw royalty worthy of imitation for how to carry yourself with style and grandeur.

Like any person of greatness, Craig found heroes. He took from those around him, watched, remembered, and internalized what would serve him in his life. And, eventually, Craig himself became a legend, hero, and myth.

In fact, still to this day, Craig is known by many from his reputation established on the streets of LA. While Craig may play down some of the impact he had on those who congregated around him, he was the recognized leader of the group known as the Avenues. Many formal historians of gangs and informal experts classify the Avenues as the precursor to the infamous Crip gang. Yet, the story is more nuanced.

Craig formed the set in 1965, sitting in front of an olive tree on a street corner near the intersection of 82nd and Hooper Avenue. The name itself came from the street sign "Hooper Avenue." The development of the gang filled a vacuum left by many of the older gangs in the area being "played out." Older gang members were either incarcerated or moving past their gangbanging days.

To think about the Avenues as simply a gang may give the group a greater sense of criminality than it actually merits. The Avenues were a group of kids brought together by friendship and a communal commitment to getting stronger together.

Their clubhouse was a weight room, their primary activity was working out, and their primary goal was looking like the bodybuilders filling the pages of the muscle magazines stacked against the wall.

Like so many young men, adolescent Monson was looking for inspiration, for a hero, for strength. Sure, he found role models in and around his neighborhood. But the strength he was seeking was beyond that. In the magazines overflowing the garage gym, he found pages filled with heroes of strength.

Craig was mesmerized by strength.

As a kid, Craig would save his weekly allowance to buy *Iron Man* physical culture magazines. Inside the magazines, he found images of the top bodybuilders of the time, and they became inspirations.

Already a nascent artist, Monson started putting images of strength on paper by drawing muscled gladiators and Vikings armed with swords.

Craig brought those drawings to life when he found his way to the weights. He was introduced to his relationship with weightlifting by Johnny Boy. A few years older than Craig, Johnny Boy had a weight pile on his front yard. Along with his friend Raymond Burns, Johnny Boy had a crude but effective training setup with some milk crates and two by fours. A couple of years later, Johnny Boy would be the first guy from the neighborhood to be drafted during Vietnam. Unfortunately, Johnny Boy never made it back home, but he left Craig with an introduction to the iron that would forever change his life.

Craig started to look frantically for ways and places to train. Although the gym at Charles Drew Junior High School had only a simple Universal gym setup, Monson would spend hours on the machine. Craig recalls that there was no cable setup on the machine, but there was a leg press, a pull-up bar, and a bench press. Bodybuilding was far from a mainstream pursuit at that time, and school administration began to take notice of Craig's "unusual" fixation on working out. Then, when they find his muscle drawings and magazines in his locker during a routine locker inspection, Craig's parents were notified. Concerned about a possible emotional imbalance, the vice principal explained the situation to Monson's mom and stepdad.

Craig's mom looked past the seeming concern of school officials and saw her son's rugged determination. In support of that, she bought a 13-year-old Craig his first weight set, an iron bar, and cement-filled plastic plates. With his own iron pile, Craig started to notice demonstrable results. At 14 years old, Craig needed to cut slits into his shirtsleeves to make room for his bulging biceps. At 16 years old, he would cause car accidents when drivers became distracted at the sight of a shirtless Monson with his massive physique.

Craig's gains were tracked annually by the continual growth in the circumference of his arms. As he explains it, at 15 he developed 15-inch arms, at 16 he developed 16-inch arms, at 17 he had 17-inch arms, at 18 he had 18-inch arms, and this kept going so that by the time Craig hit the exercise yard at the state prison in Tracy, California, at 21 years old, his rolled-up sleeves revealed legitimate 21-inch guns.

As Craig became more devoted to the iron, he enlisted the help of a friend who worked as a welder at a shipyard to design workout equipment to his particular specifications. As a foundation for his growing gym in his mom's backyard, Craig mixed and poured 11 yards of concrete.

However, during these early years of Craig's life, the most impactful training location was the gym he shared with his friends. From childhood through his time in the penal system and his time as a bodybuilder on into later in his life, Craig's best friend, wingman, and most trusted confidant was Donny Boy. And it was at Donny Boy's house where they built their gym.

The workout setup was a bit crude but efficient and a source of great pride for the young men. The weight stack was mostly "dimes." They had a bench press with a ceiling mirror facing down on the bench, so the guys could see all the flexing chesticles at work. An old heavy bag, which hung listlessly in the corner, would come alive once someone started banging away on it. Craig remembers hitting the bag with such youthful zeal and ferocity that the very building would shudder in response.

It was in this context that Craig first developed his work ethic, discipline, and complete commitment to his relationship with the weights.

Every time he worked out, Craig's goal was to have a pool of sweat collecting at his feet. Craig's conviction in this garage gym was so earnest that he requested no distractions and would not allow any needless horseplay. This mindset led to one of the more intriguing incidents of LA street folklore.

When conversations at social functions or casual exchanges turn to the topic of street gangs, the name that rings the loudest is the infamous Crips. Now, online discussion forums and gang experts all offer different opinions regarding the backstory of the name *Crips*.

Craig explains the genesis of the gang can be traced back to an incident at the Avenue's gym. On one occasion, Craig was going through his workout routine with his usual fierce intensity, which was becoming customary and expected by those around him. However, on that particular day, not everyone at the garage weight pile was a member of the Avenues.

In the pantheon of LA OGs, few names carry the weight of Raymond Washington. Born and raised in South Central, early on Raymond developed a reputation as someone who was good with his hands. As the older gangs of the Businessmen, Gladiators, and Slausons gave way to the empowerment movement surrounding the Black Panther Party, there was a vacuum to be filled by younger gangs. The Avenues, whose primary activities revolved around working out and who consisted of a select group of close friends, was not large enough of an entity to fill that space. Enter Raymond Washington and his gang, the Crips. Started by Raymond Washington in 1969, the Crips initially formed on the east side of South Central. The gang gained membership and momentum in 1971, when Washington united his gang with a group on the west side of South Central under the leadership of Stanley "Tookie" Williams. From there, Crip gangs reached across LA, and later they would spread throughout the United States.

Before being the initial spark for a gang that spread like a wildfire, on one particular day, Raymond was a teenage kid watching the older members of the Avenues go through their workout. While Craig was performing his routine with his trademark intensity, Raymond started in on a series of "yo mama" jokes. At first, Craig brushed it off. But, when the incessant jesting continued, Craig leaned over to Donny Boy and told him that Raymond better knock that stuff off.

Unabated, Raymond kept on.

Unabashedly, Craig leaned over, reached back, and hit Raymond with an open hand, a slap.

Although not a closed fist, a strike from a young, pumped-up Big Craig Monson carried plenty of power, and it, unsurprisingly, put Raymond down. When he got up, he was sniffling and limping (from an old injury to his leg).

Craig was succinct in his dismissal, "Get out of here you 'crip,'" in reference to Raymond's "crippled" leg.

"I'm going to start my own gang," Raymond said in an attempt of slight defiance.

"Oh, yeah?" Craig said incredulously. "What are you going to call the gang? The Crips?"

Thus, the origin story of the Crips.

While the trajectory of LA street gang would forever be changed with this incident, Craig's life would unfold in another direction because of a different incident.

As a teenager, Craig found himself falling into habitual criminal offenses. His first incarceration was a relatively brief 14½ weeks at Camp William Mendenhall juvenile detention center.

Back out, the following year Craig was walking out of Kitchen liquor store on the corner of Firestone and Central when he got into a beef with an older guy. Things escalated and the man reached inside his jacket. At 18, Monson was already a veteran of street violence. With this experience, Craig knew that you don't wait to find out what is going to be pulled out. You have to act and do it with conviction. Rather than waiting to see if the guy was pulling a piece or a blade, Craig rifled his punch down the pipe and laid out the guy. That act of perceived self-preservation got him 90 days in County on assault. The year after that, Craig was at Wayside Honor Rancho (now Peter J. Pitchess Detention Center) for four months on a burglary charge.

Then, in 1970, a man broke into Craig's mother's house. As Monson explains it, with clear objectivity afforded by the passage of time, Craig tussled with the intruder briefly, before the burglar hit Craig with a ball peen hammer, causing Craig to falter. Shaking off the blow,

Craig seized the hammer and set about beating the robber. He kept hitting him until the guy was done. He was dead.

As a consequence, Craig's life would be changed forever.

In a clear act of defense but without adequate legal representation, Craig was found guilty of manslaughter. This verdict got Craig a ticket to some of the hardest correctional facilities: first, the "gladiator school" at Tracy and then off to the infamous San Quentin. Behind bars, Craig would meet new mentors, face new challenges, and attain a new level of physical, mental, and emotional strength. He would also find a way to use his strength as a means to improve his plight.

THE WORKOUT

Classic rock, classic cars, classic movies, and classic physiques. That was the best of the 1960s, and Big Craig Monson epitomized the bodybuilding look of the era, a time when the sport was dominated by "The Myth" Sergio Oliva, Larry Scott, and Harold Poole.

Like a true classic, the look is timeless and revered, and, regardless of what contemporary armchair lifting pundits say, it's the look still most admired in bodybuilding circles. This physique was capped with fully rounded pecs, biceps that peak like the Himalayas, and breathtaking back arms.

A laser-like focus on the chest and arms is required to build this physique. Like a weightlifting monk, Craig took on this vow without deviation. His routine was tough, and the workload in one of his training sessions was more than many men do in a month.

Craig's routine was real and raw. And, you are about to see exactly what Craig did.

If you are brave enough to attempt this routine, make sure you are in a caloric surplus, well rested, and ready to get after it.

The routine requires no fancy equipment or space-age machines, and it built Big Craig's 21-inch arms, totally drug-free.

Monday (Day 1)/Friday (Day 5)

Exercise	Sets	Reps	Weight	Rest Interval
Push-Ups against the Wall	3	25-30	Bodyweight	60 sec
Bench Press	8	8-12	Heavy as possible	120 sec
Incline Bench Press	6	8-12	Heavy as possible	120 sec
Flat Dumbbell Bench Press	4-6	6-8	Heavy as possible	60 sec
Dumbbell Fly Massive Stretches	4	8-10	Light	60 sec
Champagnes Flat Bench	4	8-10	Moderate	60 sec
Bent-Over Rows	4	8	Moderate	90 sec
One-Arm Dumbbell Rows	4	8	Heavy	60 sec
Bent-Arm EZ Curl Bar Pullovers	4	8	Moderate	60 sec
Straight-Arm Dumbbell Pullovers	4	8-10	Moderate	60 sec

Special Notes

Push-Ups against the Wall: These are done just to get a slight pump and blood flow; fatigue is not the goal.

Bench Press: Go as heavy as possible; the goal is straight sets. Set one, in the best-case scenario, is the same weight as set eight. Very similar to German Volume training, albeit Craig was doing this training in the 1960s.

Incline Bench Press: Go as heavy as possible; the goal is straight sets. Set one, in the best-case scenario, is the same weight as set six.

Flat Dumbbell Bench Press: Go as heavy as possible; the goal is straight sets.

Dumbbell Fly Massive Stretches: Craig picked up the dumbbells off the floor while lying on a flat bench (not a typo). While the emphasis was on stretch and feel, Craig eventually worked up to 100 pounds in each hand. Craig kept the reps neutral-grip at the top of the movement, but as he descended, he would turn his arms so the end of the bell would touch the floor. These were always about a stretch and feel, not heavy weight.

Champagnes are a prison yard favorite, and a finishing touch Craig used to build the biggest hood in the hood! Champagnes are executed by grabbing a pair of dumbbells and lying on a flat bench. From this spot, position the dumbbells together. Craig would rotate his hands backward so that his pinkies were above his thumbs. From here, Craig would press the weight up and back to the starting point; keep in mind the negative portion of the rep was like pouring champagne, hence the name. Once in a while, Craig would do this prison yard favorite on an incline for the sake of variation. The focus here was on intentional contraction of the inner chest, not moving heavy pig iron.

Bent-Over Barbell Rows were performed with moderate weight, with the focus being on contraction of the upper back muscles, not bar weight.

One-Arm Dumbbell Rows were performed as heavy as possible for four sets of eight reps. Craig's opposing hand and knee were on the opposing side contrasted to his work side.

Bent-Arm Pullovers were performed with a barbell and a 30-degree bend in the elbow. The emphasis here was the stretch, not heavy weight. This was done to "expand the rib cage" by building the intercostals and creating the illusion of a bigger, fuller chest. Craig focused on purposeful chest contractions.

Straight-Arm Dumbbell Pullovers were executed by Craig lying sideways across a bench, making sure his hips were lower than his shoulders, with his arms in full extension. The emphasis here was the stretch, not heavy weight.

Tuesday (Day 2)/Thursday (Day 4)

Exercise	Sets	Reps	Weight	Rest Interval
Curls	2	25	Light	60 sec
Back Arms (Triceps Extensions)	8	8-12	Heavy	90 sec
Straight Bar Curls	6-8	8-12	Heavy as possible, strict	90 sec
One-Arm Dumbbell Concentration Curls	4	15	Light/moderate	60 sec
45-Degree Preacher Curls	4-6	8-15	Heavy	75 sec
Dumbbell Extensions behind the Head	4	8-10	Moderate	60 sec
Lying Dumbbell Extensions	4-6	8-12	Moderate	60 sec
Wrist Curls	4-6	50	Moderate	

Curls were performed very light to warm up the elbows and with just the bar. Craig always used a straight bar because that is all he had; the straight bar, however, forced his arms to remain in supination, forcing his biceps to work overtime.

Back Arms (Triceps Extensions): Craig did the first two sets in a style where he lifted the barbell away from his head and moved it horizontally or parallel to the floor. From here, Craig worked up as heavy as possible over the next six sets, in a strict traditional style, with the weight moving up and down in the vertical plane.

Straight Bar Curls were strict but as heavy as possible with a goal of using the same weight across all the sets.

One-Arm Dumbbell Concentration Curls: Craig grabbed a dumbbell with one hand and sat on the edge of a bench, placing his feet wider than shoulder-width. From here, he placed the back of his arm with the dumbbell on the inside of his thigh and placed his opposite hand on top of his opposite knee for support. Then he executed intentional, slow, controlled reps with every ounce of his being focused on his biceps.

45 Degree Preacher Curls were strict but as heavy as possible with a goal of using the same weight across all the sets. Focus on the "pump" and a good "feel."

Craig next supersetted **dumbbell extensions behind the head** with the concentration curls. After raising the dumbbell above his head until his arms were fully extended, Craig would slowly lower the weight, grabbing it by the end of the bell, back behind his head, really focusing on the stretch. He would do the movement stretching to the right side of his head and then to the left in an alternating fashion.

Next up, Craig did **dumbbell triceps extensions while lying down** on a flat bench. He used a neutral grip the entire time, and the focus was the triceps contraction, not heavy weight.

Triceps extensions were supersetted with **wrist curls,** seated and as heavy as possible, with his forearms supinated resting on his thighs.

Wednesday

This day is the same as Monday/Friday except for one major notable exception on bench press. This day, Craig did "pull sets." A **pull set** is very similar to a drop set.

In this workout, Craig would start off with bench press for two sets of 8 to 12 reps, as heavy as possible. From there, he would work up a set of three to four reps as heavy as possible. Once Craig hit muscle failure, he would rest the bar on his chest, and two competent spotters that he trusted with his life would proceed to pull a plate off each side. From here, Craig would pump out as many reps as he could. When he was again at failure, he would rest the bar on his chest, and the spotters would pull a plate off each side, and Craig would continue until he could go no more.

Craig would rest five minutes and do it again. On overly ambitious days, he would repeat this sequence thrice.

A pull set differs from a drop set because weight is stripped at the bottom of the movement and the weight is never racked! You are under tension the entire time.

After bench press, the rest of the session would be the same as Monday and Friday.

Thursday (Every Other Week)

Twice a month, Craig took his arm workout to an entirely new level of intensity and overload.

This session consisted of pull sets on curls, exactly as described in the bench press. However, these curls were cheat curls! Craig cheated the weight up and lowered it at a controlled pace; cheating, in this case, was not used to cut corners but to make the training harder and provide "the knots" with an overload they would not experience otherwise! This was similar to the way Arnold, Sergio, and Ronnie Coleman "cheated."

Next, Craig would go into his legendary **"three-quarter" curls**. Like Craig's pull technique, he would never set the bar down. Craig would put three 25-pound plates (quarters) on each side of a straight bar; he would curl this for five reps, then his partners would strip a quarter off each side of the bar, and Craig would bang out 10 reps with two quarters. Next, Craig would reverse his hands on the barbell after his partners reduced the weight to one quarter on each side and he'd bust out 15 reverse curls. Finally, Craig would flip his hands back around and perform 20 curls with as narrow of a grip as possible. This was done three times!

Craig would finish the day with high-rep back arms. Craig would warm up with two moderate weight sets of triceps extensions, then he would do five sets of six to eight reps on triceps extensions. Adding weight each set, he would make sure the final two sets were finished with forced reps. Craig preferred to have the spotter's hands on his hands for the forced reps.

This was done in place of the normal Thursday workout.

Craig says it is very important to have a great spotter on this day, one with the heart of a lion. Your spotter needs to be someone who makes you thrive and wants you to succeed to maximize this training session.

Final Thoughts

The rest periods are an educated guess, as oftentimes it came down to who was changing plates and alternating with Craig on the exercises. The attitude was one of intentional focus. Playing grab ass was forbidden (as Raymond Washington quickly learned after Craig slapped him upside the head for squirrelling around in the weight room).

Craig's routine built arguably the most well-developed, natural set of chest and arms in the history of bodybuilding. So, take note and be forewarned, this routine is not for the faint of heart.

Chapter Two

THE STORY

In the second stage of his development, Craig led with strength. Incarceration can be a tumultuous and upending experience. As a means to maintain emotional equilibrium, various tools are utilized behind bars. Some inmates turn to education for intellectual enrichment, some use religion for spiritual enlightenment, and others take drugs to just drift away.

Unsurprisingly, Craig's preferred tool for this period of tribulation was strength. Specifically, strength training. As soon as he hit LA County Jail, he started on his daily calisthenics routine of push-ups, bodyweight squats, dips, and an improvised rowing movement with a towel and his bunk bed frame.

Now, along with being really clear about staying with his workout routine, Craig was also unwavering in his position among the other inmates. As he put it, he was a "hog" (you know, a heavyweight, someone with brass balls, the alpha male). The sleeping quarters were set up in a communal fashion. In that sort of arrangement, there would be plenty of dudes who would be worried about their security and, as a consequence, shirk away from any potential confrontation. Looking to not be noticed, they would just intend to get through the situation intact.

Unfortunately, in that type of predatory environment, disinclination toward conflict is seen as a characteristic of those who will become prey. While some attempt to hide away their insecurity and fear with loud barks of bravado, others don't act as anything but prey.

But Craig was a hog through and through, yes he was. Not only did he immediately start in on his lengthy workout of hundreds of reps of bodyweight training, but he commanded everyone in his unit to work out with him. From the get-go, Craig let the institution know that Big Monson had arrived.

Part coach and part training partner, Craig led his fellow inmates in a tortuous routine of calisthenics. Now, anyone with experience in working out knows the importance of a workout partner. You will lift more weight, stay in the gym longer, hit more reps, and be more focused when you have someone training alongside you.

With this in mind, part of the reason Craig wanted everyone around him going through the same routine was because it would push him to train harder. In County or not, Craig had every intention to keep training hard. Like in his teenage days with his fellow Avenue members alongside him, in County, Craig created a camaraderie around strength and getting stronger.

Not only was Craig strengthened through this process of communal workout, but those around him were empowered as well. Like a jailhouse preacher, Craig was bringing the gospel of strength. This message and practice would accompany Craig throughout his sojourn in the penal system. And as he progressed in this journey, it served him well.

Built in 1963, Men's Central Jail houses inmates who are awaiting trial or have been convicted of crimes. After he was convicted of manslaughter for killing the home invader, County Jail was just a transitional place for Craig.

Ultimately, Monson was sent to the infamous Deuel Vocational Institution in San Joaquin County, California. Although named for California state senator Charles H. Deuel, the facility is commonly known as Tracy, due to its proximity to the city of the same name. Among convicts and prison staff, Tracy was known for many years as the "gladiator school" because of the sheer prevalence of fights, stabbings, and killings, all of which Craig would be exposed to during his tenure at this facility.

In the nefarious saga of prison gang folklore, Tracy is known as the place of origin of the notorious Mexican Mafia, established in 1956.

In the empowering myth of prison lifting, Tracy was the place where Big Craig Monson made his presence known in the iron pit.

When Craig got off the bus at Tracy, one of the first things he noticed was the large weight pile in the middle yard. In the midst of a place filled with much despair and sadness, this immediately lifted his spirits. While the bodyweight workouts at County were filling his emotional need for training and developing his muscular endurance, Craig the hog was missing some pig iron.

However, not everyone at Tracy was granted access to the main workout facility in the yard, and no one got immediate access. The deal was that each prisoner had to get a card to access the good weights. On Saturday, there was a tryout, of sorts, where you could earn the card if you hit 300 pounds on the bench press. Since Craig arrived at Tracy at the beginning of the week, he had to work out with the scrap weights until he could show his strength. Well, at the next try-out day, show his strength he did by easily repping out 300 pounds for a set of 10. Easily passing the test and announcing his arrival on the yard, Craig was now a member of the pit.

Once he got access to some heavy iron, Craig got his workout crew in order. His lifting partners were Larry Armstead, known as "Big Youngster," Terry Bradshaw, known as "Big Bradshaw," Cartwright, who was very country, and Bittersweet, who was a bit of a playboy and therefore preferred a leaner, more defined look than the rest of the crew.

Then as now, inmates in the California penal system self-segregate along race and, to a lesser extent, along geographic divides. Most generally, white inmates congregate with other white inmates, black inmates with other black inmates, and Mexican inmates with other Mexican inmates. The less significantly represented ethnicities (like Asians, Polynesians, and Native Americans) ride together in smaller "cars," or groups. The divisions separating racial intermixing are strict and closely guarded. Stepping over these boundaries can lead to beatdowns, stabbings, or large-scale rioting.

Now, there are some people who say that love transcends color. And that is true. However, in the penal system, strength transcends racial boundaries. Big boys respect big boys. While he was not able to form close friendships with lifters of other races, Craig found mutual respect with lifters outside of his immediate circle.

One such lifter was a big white dude with blond hair, worn long in both the style of the time and that of the rebel biker, who went by the name of Sunshine. A member of the Hell's Angels, the feared outlaw biker gang, Sunshine and Monson came from diametrically opposed worlds. But they shared a passion for the pig iron. Strength transcends color.

Years later, when Craig was out of prison and driving his 1978 Corvette on his way to a Sunday morning workout at the pit, he stopped to eat at Norm's in Santa Monica. Out front was a long line of chopper-style bikes. The leather cuts adorning the tattooed bikers announced their affiliation with the outlaw motorcycle lifestyle.

Craig walked with an unbroken stride past the bikers, focused on a bulking meal before a long workout. Then he heard a booming voice shout to him from among the leather, ink, and long hair.

"Big Truck is that you?!"

Using Craig's nickname from his time inside, there was Sunshine reaching out to greet his brother of strength. The friendship endured both sides of prison walls and racial divides because real recognizes real, strength respects strength, and hogs know they are hogs.

The nickname "Big Truck" was given to Craig partially because of his massive size, but also because he was willing to roll over anyone in his way. In fact, it was Craig's friendship with another inmate from a different race, and his willingness to smash (like something from monster truck madness) anyone who would threaten his friend, that got him transferred from Tracy after a 90-day stay.

A small Mexican kid from Craig's old neighborhood was also serving time at Tracy. Craig remembered that this kid's grandma introduced him to tacos and his sister was fine, a real beauty. Behind bars, the kid got caught up in some politics and became a target. Friendship is not something Craig takes lightly, and he stood up. The decision he made and the action he took resulted in Craig getting transferred to San Quentin.

On the bus ride from Tracy to Quentin, Craig took a cursory look around at his fellow convicts. Like a prescribed ritual, inmate after inmate took a lit cigarette to various tattoos, erasing visible signs of gang affiliations that could be detrimental to their survival inside the complex labyrinth of prison tribal divisions. Craig knew then that Quentin would be the next level of incarceration and house a whole different type of convict.

In fact, Craig was mentored by some of the most infamous at Quentin. Similar to his experiences on the streets, Monson gravitated toward fellow men of strength.

There are some people whose life reads like something from an adventure novel. Elmer "Geronimo" Pratt served two combat tours in Vietnam as a long-range reconnaissance expert with the Army's 82nd Airborne Division. Rising to the rank of sergeant, he earned two Bronze Stars, a Silver Star, and two Purple Hearts. Upon leaving the service, Pratt moved to Los Angeles, where he studied political science at UCLA and caught the eye of the Black Panther Party leadership. Upon his recruitment to the Party by Bunchy Carter and activist John Huggins, Pratt rose quickly to the position of Deputy Minister of Defense, took the name "Geronimo" (after the Chiricahua Apache chief by the same name), and, under the orders of Newton, went underground to build a revolutionary infrastructure for the achievement of a separate black nation.

As a consequence of his revolutionary activity, first the LAPD and later the FBI began to surveil Geronimo. This attention from law enforcement resulted in Pratt being hit with a murder and kidnapping charge relating to a 1968 robbery on a Santa Monica tennis court. Proclaiming his innocence, Geronimo hired the lawyer Johnnie Cochran (who would later receive publicity for his defense of O.J. Simpson). However, an informant inside of the Black Panthers, infighting among Party leadership, and dubious actions taken by the FBI's covert counterintelligence program, COINTELPRO, prevented the proof of Geronimo's innocence. Pratt spent 27 years in prison and, refusing to renounce his politics or admit guilt, was turned down for parole 16 times.

Finally, on June 10, 1997, Pratt's conviction was vacated (which makes a previous judgment legally void) after it was revealed that the prosecution concealed evidence, and Pratt was released the following month. Johnnie Cochran's law firm, The Cochran Firm, filed a lawsuit against the FBI and the LAPD, which was settled for $4.5 million.

Geronimo spent the initial eight years of his prison sentence at San Quentin, where he took Craig under his wing. Sitting alongside one another on the yard, Geronimo would school Craig. The two men came from the same "immigrant" experience. That is, both were black men who were born in the Deep South (Louisiana in the case of Pratt and Arkansas in the case of Monson) and migrated west with dreams of sunnier shores in palm tree–clad Los Angeles. Unfortunately, the reality of that dream resulted in them sharing time at San Quentin.

Having studied at the University of California along with the curriculum of the streets, jungle warfare, and, now, the penal system, Geronimo had crammed a lot of learning into a relatively short period of living. He was only 24 years old at the time.

In the realm of formal education, Geronimo urged, even insisted, that Craig complete high school while incarcerated, which he did.

In the more subtle areas of interpersonal relationships and emotional intelligence, Geronimo was not just a casual people watcher. He was an observer of humanity in all of its strange and fascinating behavior—a skill set that he passed along to Craig. He would tell Craig to pick one convict and watch him all day. Observe his behavior. Pay attention to how he handles himself. Be alert to things he does and says, but also the more subtle but equally important nonverbal cues. Notice and remember the signs of aggression, passivity, and deception. All these things can be witnessed and learned with a constant and critical eye.

Geronimo remained alert in a manner that armchair therapists would refer to as paranoia, but seasoned street soldiers would call hypervigilance. Well before a global pandemic necessitated such precaution, Pratt advocated keeping a social distance from people. He advised Monson to remain at least three feet from fellow convicts. This space would reduce the likelihood of being the recipient of a roughly made prison shiv, or at least give the target time to respond with sufficient force.

Lessons like these stuck with Craig as he made his way through the penal system and eventually found himself on the other side of prison walls.

While they may have lacked the eclectic experiences of Geronimo, Craig's days at Quentin were filled with meeting many other notorious convicts and convict organizations, such as Wesley Robert Wells, who spent nearly half a century under lock and key. A black man who grew up as an orphan, Wells was first sent to Quentin at 19 for receiving a stolen suit of clothes. Once inside, he become a product of the institution and the harsh realities of that particular environment. In 1931, Wells was convicted of manslaughter for the stabbing death of a fellow inmate. Later he was sentenced to death after he hurled a spittoon at a guard. His case became a cause célèbre for a broken legal system. Finally, Wells was released in 1974, his body ravaged by ulcers and arthritis, while his mind was anguished by years of unjust imprisonment.

While not as famous in the free world, behind bars Nelson Anderson had a fearsome reputation. A black convert to Islam, Anderson and all of his Muslim Brothers kept a strict decorum of discipline and dressed in a uniform of peacoats. A serious adherent of strength routines, Anderson had 20-inch arms. When he and Craig were locked up together at LA County and then later at San Quentin, the two of them would bang out push-ups by the hundreds. Differences in approaches to religion aside, a mutual appreciation for training brought together these convicts.

As much as strength can bring people together, it also takes strength to keep some people at bay. It takes strength to build and maintain boundaries. In any relationship—platonic, romantic, and professional—boundaries are important. Certainly, strong boundaries are important inside of prison. As Geronimo taught Craig, you need to be cautious about the people you let close. This is valuable advice for anyone, no matter on which side of a guard tower they live.

Be vigilant about whom you let into your inner circle.

In an atmosphere where everyone has an angle, a hustle, and a plot, you need to be constantly on guard. However, prison has many of the features of a Hobbesian state of nature, and in such a setting you need some sort of a support system. As strong as you are, you need someone backing you up.

Ethnic divisions are guarded closely in prison. Inmates stay "with their own" for many reasons, but one of the most prominent concerns is fear of gang retribution. Anxiety about a gang from another race making a move against you usually takes a back seat to the more immediate awareness that one wrong step could result in a stomping, or worse, from the clique inside of your own race. One of the primary activities of any prison gang is keeping their "own people" in line. Ironically, the flagship gang of each race was started with the intended goal of protecting their race from predation. Unsurprisingly, considering that each group is primarily made up of hardened criminals, the primary focus of the movement has shifted away from self-preservation and toward the creation and perpetuation of a criminal organization.

So, while prison gangs were largely started with the stated intent of self-defense, they quickly formed into sophisticated bands of organized crime.

One such group was the Black Guerilla Family, also known as the "BGF." Fueled by the Black Nationalist writings of Marcus Garvey, the BGF saw itself as a Black Marxist-Maoist revolutionary movement with the aims of achieving dignity for black inmates and shaking off the fetters of the oppressive American government. Founded in 1966 by George Jackson and W.L. Nolan at San Quentin, the BGF quickly became a powerful voice in the Black Power movement, beyond bars and on the street. As authentic as the political and racial ideology may have initially been, the BGF morphed rapidly into a violent criminal organization.

If for no other reason, the sheer size and power of the BGF caused many young black inmates to join and become absorbed into this sprawling gang. However, Craig was different. More so than most, Craig was physically strong. Unlike most, he also possessed a powerful sense of self and the direction he wanted his life to take. He knew that he didn't want to get lost in the trap of prison politics, which only lead to a later release date or perhaps never being a free man again. No, Craig was committed to leaving prison and walking out a stronger man than when he came in.

When a new inmate hits the yard, they are often met by a member of one of the major gangs representing their particular ethnicity. The rep may give a rundown of the rules and politics currently in place at that particular institution. They will also look to recruit a new inmate to "put in work," or do the bidding (from smuggling contraband to carrying out hits) of the gang.

With Craig the situation was distinct. When a member of the BGF approached Monson, he came with a specific agenda. Craig's strength was obvious, and the BGF looked to bring him on board to be strengthened through him. They proposed to make him a "general."

As a supporter of the Black Panther Party movement in Los Angeles, Craig was receptive to the stated ideological aims of the BGF. At the same time, Craig was astute enough to know that those were distinct from the actual criminal behavior of the group. Joining this organization meant becoming complicit in certain illicit deeds. That was not the path Craig envisioned for his life. He did not want to become a career criminal.

So, Monson rejected the offer, forcibly.

It was that strength of body, character, and personality that Craig took with him through his time of incarceration and that he brought with him once released.

THE WORKOUT

In the 1970s, there was a war going on, and the theater was the California State Penitentiary. This war didn't end with one, two, or even 10 tours of duty. Amongst Craig Monson and his training part- ners, every day was a new battle with pig iron over who would be the "hog," or alpha male, of the weight pit.

Before 1992, when California banned weights in prisons, serious lifting was common in prisons. And Big Craig Monson blazed a trail of strength and hard training that many cons emulated.

On the yard, Craig and his workout partners did not have access to Clorox-cleaned chrome machines, famous personal trainers, or any of the so-called modern-day advances that characterize the workouts of contemporary bodybuilding enthusiasts in their plush private gym settings.

What they did have access to was bare-bones, basic, raw pig iron.

Craig's jaw-dropping physique built behind bars was built 100 per- cent drug free. Rather than turning to chemistry, the recipe was heavy weight with copious amounts of volume. Simply put, Craig did more in a workout than most gym newbies and weightlifting neophyte trainees do in a month.

While Craig's routine seems pretty basic, it was brutally effective. By the time Craig checked out of the "crowbar hotel," he had more size and strength than the juiced professional bodybuilders of the day.

When Craig first arrived at Tracy Correctional Institution, not only did he immediately earn the right to slang iron in the pit, but he became the favorite candidate for the title of "Pit Hog." Prior to Craig's arrival, the usual suspects had their established workout routines. But Craig, the new guy, quickly built a reputation. So, while his teachings disrupted the status quo, they were embraced and brought an effective, results-oriented training plan to the state pen.

Now, the current trend in corporate America is to strive toward creating a safe space and comfortable environment. The weight pit in the California Penal System in the 1970s was the polar opposite: a gladiator-like hierarchy where alpha males thrived and beta males knew their place. There was no human resources department, just brutal beatdowns if you did not toe the company line, where Craig was CEO.

Like any great leader, Monson knew that great accomplishments come when you have a great team. Craig attributes much of his training success at Tracy and San Quentin to his training partners.

There were four total; any more slowed down the pace. The training tempo remained high. Rest periods were minimal because inmates had an hour to get all of their training done. Too many bodies slowed down the pace, and someone who was weak required way too much plate changing. Plus, Craig knew if he ran with the lame, eventually he would develop a limp. The OGs of the pit, Craig's training partners included Cartwright, Bradshaw, and Big Youngster.

In Tracy, Craig's routine consisted of the following:

Monday

Exercise	Sets	Reps	Weight	Rest Interval
Incline Bench Press	4-5	5-8	Heavy as possible	See description
Bench Press	4-5	8-12	Heavy as possible	See description
Flat Dumbbell Bench Press	4-6	6-8	Heavy as possible	See description
Incline Dumbbell Bench Press	4	10-15	Heavy as possible	See description
Dumbbell Fly Massive Stretches	4	10-12	Light	See description
Bent-Over Barbell Rows	4	8-12	Moderate	See description
One Arm Dumbbell Rows	4	8-20	Heavy as possible	See description

Special Notes

Rest Intervals: Craig would go and then his partners would go; then they would start over. No downtime as time was of the essence on the yard. This was on everything unless otherwise noted.

Incline Bench Press: Go as heavy as possible; the goal is straight sets. Set one, in the best-case scenario, is the same weight as sets four to five. Craig preferred bench press first but was willing to compromise with his training partners. Eventually he worked up to reppin' six quarters like Big Youngster.

Bench Press: Go as heavy as possible; the goal is straight sets. Set one, in the best-case scenario, is the same weight as set five.

Flat Dumbbell Bench Press: Go as heavy as possible; the goal is straight sets.

Incline Dumbbell Bench Press: Go as heavy as possible; the goal is straight sets.

Dumbbell Fly Massive Stretches: Craig picked up the dumbbells off the floor while lying on a flat bench (not a typo). While the emphasis was on stretch and feel, Craig eventually worked up to 100 pounds in each hand. Craig kept the reps neutral-grip at the top of the movement, but as he descended, he would turn his arms so the end of the bell would touch the floor. These were always about a stretch and feel, not heavy weight. Craig's partners were not thrilled about flys, but once they saw their effectiveness, they jumped on board.

Bent-Over Barbell Rows were performed with moderate weight, with the focus being on contraction of the upper-back muscles, not bar weight.

One-Arm Dumbbell Rows were performed as heavy as possible for four sets of eight to twenty reps. Craig's opposing hand and knee were on the opposing side contrasted to his work side.

Tuesday

Yard days were limited, so this was a rest day. This rest day consisted of sets of 25 push-ups, with a 500-mandatory minimum. Craig could see Bradshaw from his second-tier cell, and Craig would make eye contact with Bradshaw and then execute 25 push-ups. After this, he would nod to Bradshaw, and Bradshaw would bang out 25 reps. They went back and forth until 500 or more push-ups were eclipsed.

Wednesday

Craig and company would attack this day with a Zeus-like energy because they felt well rested after not having access to weights on Tuesday.

After a warm-up of 25 reps with 100 pounds on biceps curls, the following routine ensued.

Exercise	Sets	Reps	Weight	Rest Interval
Straight Bar Curls	10	10-1	125	See above description
Back Arms (Triceps Extensions)	4-5	8-10	Heavy as possible	See above description
Cheat Curls	4	10	Heavy as possible	See above description
Triceps Extensions	4-6	6-8	Heavy as possible	Superset Curls
Dumbbell Shotguns	4	10-12	Light	See above description
Seated Military Press	4	10-12	Heavy as possible	See above description
Seated behind the Neck Press	4	10-12	Heavy as possible	See above description
Seated Front Raises	4	8-12	Moderate	See above description
Seated Lateral Raises	4	8-12	Light	See above description
Upright Rows	4	8-12	Moderate	See above description
Barbell Shrugs	4	8-12	Moderate	Superset Upright Rows

Straight Bar Curls: Craig always used a straight bar because that is all he had; the straight bar, however, forced his arms to remain in supination, forcing his biceps to work overtime. Craig and just one partner would pass the bar back and forth. Craig would go, then his partner would go. Limiting it to two people allowed this to move fast. It was a one-to-one, work-to-rest ratio. A 125-pound, welded, nonadjustable barbell was used. Sets were performed in descending order from 10 and went 10,9,8,7,6,5,4,3,2,1 (for those iron game historians, this is very similar to Chuck Sipes's 1-10-1 methodology).

Back Arms (Triceps Extensions): Craig did these in a style where he lifted the barbell away from his head and moved it horizontally or parallel to the floor.

Cheat Curls: Craig used cheat curls to make the exercise harder! This was done by using just enough hip swing with a supramaximal weight to get past the limiting sticking point; from here, Craig would hold the contraction for one second at the top and intently focus on contracting his biceps. As if he were in a street fight with gravity, Craig would slowly lower the weight to the starting point, making sure to fully emphasize his biceps. Cheat curls were supersetted with triceps extensions.

Triceps Extensions here were heavy and not done in the horizontal back arms style but in the traditional strict way with the weight moving up and down in the vertical plane.

Dumbbell Triceps Shotguns: Craig would begin the movement with his hands pronated in arms extended position. Starting with his right arm (while the left arm remained in extension throughout the entire right rep), Craig would lower the dumbbell with his right arm to his left pec while his thumb was facing down. As Craig's elbow flared out perpendicular to his body, he would slightly tap his left pec. From here he would squeeze his triceps and extend the weight back to the starting position. The key was to feel the movement, not make it heavy. Craig would alternate sides doing 10-12 reps on each.

Seated Military Press: Done strict in the traditional style.

Seated behind the Neck Press: Done strict in the traditional style.

Seated Dumbbell Front Raises: Holding dumbbells, Craig would raise his arms out in front of himself until his arms were parallel to the floor, keeping a slight bend in his elbows. He would pause for a brief moment at the top of the movement, and then under control lower the dumbbells back to the starting position. Moderate weight with strict form was used.

Seated Dumbbell Lateral Raises: These were done very light in a total muscle intention style with emphasis on the side delts.

Upright Rows helped Craig build massive traps and were executed in the following manner: Craig would stand tall, holding a barbell in an overhand grip with his hands eight inches apart. From here,

Craig would raise the bar to his chin, leading with his elbows. From the top position, he slowly lowered the weight back to the starting position. Medium weight with strict form was used.

Shrugs with a barbell in a traditional style were supersetted with upright rows. Moderate weight with strict form was used.

Thursdays/Fridays

These days Craig could not get into the pit. Push-ups and other body-weight exercises were the name of the game. At least twice a week, Craig made sure to get in at least 500 reps of sit-ups, leg raises, and crunches. Everyone Craig rolled with proudly sported washboard abs.

Saturdays

This was a show-off day, meaning Craig might go ultra-heavy to establish a new personal record and reinforce that he was the Hog of the Yard. This day would also give Craig a chance to experiment with new lifts.

After Craig was transferred to San Quentin, he was able to get more days on the yard. As a result, the lifting sessions mentioned were either executed two or three times a week or Craig would do alternate workouts. For instance, he might see how many sets of bench press he could execute in an hour.

Final Thoughts

Hard, heavy, high-volume training built Craig Monson. Behind bars, you have a choice. You can essentially shorten your existence by killing time, just counting the days until your release. Or, you can make the most of your current predicament and use time as a resource. While this choice may be starker in prison, it remains true on both sides of the pen walls. Craig used time as a resource, building the physique and strength he dreamed of as a child. This consistent work ethic, as you will learn, helped Craig acquire fame and notoriety and earn a living doing what he loved.

Craig Monson training at City Gym for the 1983 Mr. World contest

Craig Monson first week back home from prison, 1974

**Craig Monson with Bradshaw, Larry Armstead
(a.k.a. Big Youngster), and Little Jimmy at San Quentin Prison, 1972**

Donnie Boy in Susanville Prison, 1972

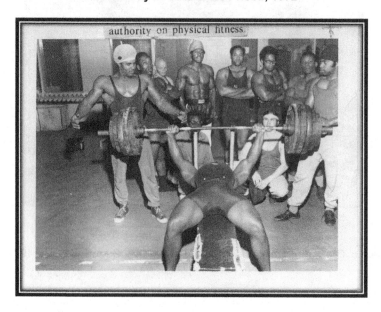

Craig Monson with Big Ben, Bad Bob, and M.L. Bridges at San Quentin Prison Gym, 1972

Craig Monson with his workout team at West Block San Quentin, 1973

Craig Monson and Pancho at Zack's Gym, 1979

Craig Monson and Pancho at Zack's Gym, 1979

Craig Monson at the age of 65 years old at Hollywood Gym

Craig Monson 19 years old at the Bucket of Blood night club on Central Avenue

Workout team West Block San Quentin, 1973

Craig Monson and Donnie Boy at San Quentin

Craig Monson on vacation in Haiti, 1976

Craig Monson with Bad Bob, Bradshaw, Hutch, and Big Youngster at San Quentin Prison, 1973

Private country club in Durango, Mexico, 1986

Craig Monson and fan Venice Beach, 1984

Craig Monson's brother, Salam, at Green Meadows Park

The Avenues Gang at Gregory Carter's (brother of Black Panther Bunchy Carter) funeral

Craig Monson with Big Squab, Eric Williams, Teddy, Pancho, Larry Hill, and Donnie Boy at Christmas party, 2016

Craig Monson at San Quentin West Block, 1973

Craig Monson and family

Craig Monson with Big Squab and Donnie Boy at Venice Beach 2017

Craig Monson with his brothers at Mavericks nightclub on Crenshaw for his 46th birthday

Craig Monson guest posing in La Canada, CA, 1984

Craig Monson's mother, Mary Alice McCuring), and his aunt, Marie Wilson, at a Los Angeles night club, 1959

Athletes Registry, Inc. **CRAIG MONSON** John Forse/Agent
A Talent Agency 2221 S. Barry Ave. Ste.200
Los Angeles, CA. 90064
213/477-8202

Gerg. Lyons/Mgr. /213/381-1682

Craig Monson hitting back arms at Venice Beach

Craig Monson posing at Pepperdine University

Chapter Three

THE STORY

In 1975, Craig Monson was released from the California penal system. Like Jean Valjean of *Les Miserables*, Monson walked out from incarceration bigger and broader. However, as an artist since his youth, Craig looked at his physique with a careful, creative, and critical eye. He was strong. He was big. He knew that he wanted a larger platform, a stage really, to display proudly the mountain of muscles he had built. Craig also knew that to be successful in bodybuilding, you needed symmetry, a certain classical development of muscularity.

For that kind of build, the rough and rugged training would get him only so far. Sure, the prison training routine would get him more powerful and build the kind of functional strength that would serve someone who needs to aggressively handle a chemically dependent interloper at the gas station off the interstate who possesses malice intent and just enough bravado to think that he found some easy prey. But a real bodybuilder needs a certain fluidity in his movement and defined lines across his physique. Of course, it should also be said that a real bodybuilder only has the luxury of refining his bulk after the groundwork is laid. Monson had put in the hours of training to get that type of powerful build which can only be developed through high-volume, heavy pig iron lifting.

So, back in LA, Craig immediately set out to find the kind of facilities where he could take his training and his rapidly developing frame to the next level. The first gym he found that suited his distinct needs was California Gym, which was located on the corner of 68th and Broadway. As any experienced gym goer and gym owner knows, sometimes the business closes. And when California Gym closed, the owner, Zach, moved the equipment to his home, where Craig would go occasionally to continue his training in a makeshift environment.

Craig ventured from training facility to training facility during this time. During periods of lengthy imprisonment, reading becomes a way to fill the hours and make the most of your time. Based on circumstance and personal inclination, the reading material varies. For Craig, it was the old paperback westerns of famous cowboy writer Louis L'Amour. Between the covers, iconic images of the old frontier came to life. The mythic description of the lone cowboy making his way in a hostile environment was an apt depiction of Craig's life in the correctional facility, where he held strong and refused to bend to the powerful winds of criminal persuasion.

Now that Monson was on the outside, the Louis L'Amour sagas continued to serve as a metaphor for the trajectory of his life. Like an old-time gunslinger, riding from town to town, Monson rode from gym to gym. He was constantly looking. He was looking for a facility that could hold up to his intensity, his strength. He was also looking for a training partner.

As every experienced lifter knows, finding the right gym can be more difficult than finding a home. And finding the right training partner can be more difficult than finding a wife.

The list of gyms Craig frequented read like the old cow towns of the west. Wyatt Earp rode from Dodge City to Tombstone. Craig trained at Trojan's Gym downtown, the YMCA, Bill Pearl's place, and Jack LaLanne's gym on Wilshire (where he didn't train for long because they only had machines, no pig iron).

After travelling from gym to gym, Monson found his place at a spot called City Gym in downtown LA (on the location now occupied by the Staples Center). He also found some training partners in Big Willie and Big Frank. With a home gym and reliable lifting partners, Monson started to make some waves, to get noticed.

Already a street legend, Craig's reputation only grew in his old hood. So much so, in fact, that some of the most notorious OGs admired Craig and actively sought out his mentorship. In the world of street gangs, few names hold the same weight as Stanley "Tookie" Williams. Working alongside Raymond Washington, Tookie was responsible for bringing together a number of independent smaller cliques and forming the multiple sets of the Crips gang, which now has an international presence and reputation. Serving as the de facto leader of the Crips for much of the 1970s, Tookie was eventually convicted of multiple murders and robberies in 1979.

Sentenced to death, Tookie's case become a cause célèbre. For instance, the rapper Snoop Dogg and actor Jamie Foxx were strident in their call for clemency for Tookie. The prominent self-help guru Tony Robbins became Tookie's close friend. Much of the attention surrounding Tookie's case grew out of the grand narrative of Williams changing from a menacing street gang leader to a children's book author who warned young people about the dangers of crime. His cinematic turnaround landed him a Nobel Prize nomination. However, even amidst the vocal efforts of the National Association for the Advancement of Colored People (NAACP) and the American Civil Liberties Union (ACLU) for a stay of execution, under California governor (and former bodybuilder) Arnold Schwarzenegger, the sentence was carried out.

Raised by a mother who was working several jobs, Tookie was a latchkey kid who took to the streets in search of belonging, direction, and mentorship. But, more than that, Tookie, like Craig, was in search of strength.

You learn things on the streets of LA. After watching grown men bet on dog fights and then having those same men bet on him when he fought other boys, Williams learned quickly that strength is a virtue. Not wanting to be a victim, he started to carry a blade pretty early on and began hanging around some of the guys who were already established in the neighborhood.

Consumed by, and focused on, his workout, Craig only vaguely remembers that Raymond Washington used to bring a young Tookie around the gym/clubhouse at Donny Boy's house. Craig was the "big dawg" for all the youngsters in the neighborhood to gawk at. The sight of Big Craig throwing around the iron left an impression on Tookie.

Arrested for car theft, Williams was sent to Los Padrinos Juvenile Hall in 1969, where he spent two years pumping the weights, following the example set for him by Big Craig Monson. By the time Tookie left the juvenile hall in 1971, Craig was away serving time. However, Tookie did not forget Monson, and his admiration for the big dawg of the neighborhood was unwavering.

So, when Craig was released in 1975, Tookie was ready to greet Monson and worked diligently to find him. Once Craig hit the streets, he was adamant that he was not going back inside, and he knew that he had to stay away from any place that would put him back behind bars. Though Craig rarely showed up back in the house, home, and hood where events conspired to send him to prison, Tookie was undeterred and would regularly stop by Craig's mom's house to inquire about him.

On the day of their memorable first encounter, Craig was sitting alongside his brother Teddy on the wall outside their mom's house when Teddy gestured down the street.

"Hey, that's Tookie right there."

Immediately, Craig could tell that Tookie was bulking himself up, with arms stretched out wide to the side like a man hauling pails full of water.

Now, Monson had just gotten out of the joint and was on a heavy bulking phase. With each step, Tookie got a better view of just how large Monson was, and the closer to Craig Tookie got, the more air came out of his carefully constructed pump-up.

At this point, they knew one another by reputation and hogs know hogs. So, Craig grabbed him in a hearty embrace, shouting, "You look like me!"

Now, both Tookie and Craig had the menacing look of a seasoned street soldier. And both were clearly devoted students of the iron. Yet, there was a difference in their size and strength. This strength divide became quite clear during one lifting session, in particular.

During the time when Monson was training at Bill Pearl's gym, Tookie would often come and lift with him on the weekend. Every time they lifted, Tookie would want to challenge Craig, to see if he could match the weights Big Monson threw around.

Three weeks before the events that landed Tookie on California's death row, they had their last workout together. It was a day when Craig decided he was going to really put it on Tookie, really go hard.

They started on bench, piling the plates on the bar until they were hitting the high 400 range. But, after benching, Tookie stepped outside to meet a white dude who was hanging out by his car. Tookie always had some sort of entourage with him, to provide backup, company, and whatever kind of support the leader of the Crips required. On this day, he was looking for a pick-me-up in the form of "Wet Daddies," or "Sherman" (embalming fluid) dipped cigarettes.

Finishing his Sherm, Tookie came back to the workout feeling superhuman. But Craig still put him through the paces. After running the weights, the two street legends agreed to a posedown. With another denizen of the hood, Gilbert Bell, judging, Craig started with a side chest shot before transitioning into a double bi pose. At each position, Gilbert would turn to Tookie and remark with a mixture of awe and good nature: "Ah, cuz, he got you."

After the workout, Tookie and Craig headed over to a hamburger stand. Monson remembers the meal vividly. He got a strawberry Crush soda, Tookie got an orange one. There they sat, all buffed up, big as a house, with cars honking at the large men as if their sheer size and muscularity made the very sight of them a performative exhibit.

In the midst of the laudatory noise and mouthfuls of hamburger, Craig passed along words which became almost prophetic in the way upcoming events made them relevant or maybe even revelatory.

Concerned about what he was hearing and seeing regarding Tookie's behavior, Craig spoke with candor: "Look, Tookie," he said, "you don't want to go where I've been."

Warning him about prison, Craig disclosed that he was still haunted by things he witnessed behind bars. Monson believed that Tookie was lighthearted; he never saw a mean streak in him. He remembers the way in which his voice was high-pitched, as if it was tuned three octaves too high.

Craig also knew that once someone started smoking that stuff, anything was possible.

Now, Craig can't, or won't, say what happened on that fateful night three weeks after their last training session, but that post-work-out meal was the last time he saw Tookie alive.

The next time he saw Tookie's face was at his wake, when Monson, with his mom at his side (Tookie was always kind to Craig's mom), looked down at the face of his friend.

Craig knew the fate waiting for so many from his old neighborhood. He knew that bodybuilding was the path and purpose that could create a different life for him. To reach that life, Craig turned himself over to the iron. Craig's dedication to bodybuilding, training, and weightlifting had the features of a monk's life. He was devoted to his craft. He lived a spartan life in diet and habits.

But, Craig had recently come out of years of incarceration. There was much of the world he hadn't seen and many things he hadn't done.

So, what do you do in Southern California when you're looking to live a little?

You head to Tijuana.

Craig and a bunch of Latino friends would head south of the border for some senoritas and margaritas. As Craig explains the setup, he was the "big black protector" to his friends, who took him from seedy "titty bars" to sandy beach cottages. After experiencing the nightlife of Revolution Avenue, Craig and friends would drive south to Rosarito Beach, where they would rent a cabin for just $26 a night.

This was living!

Craig would lie out on the beach for hours, soaking in the warm Baja California sun. Back then, you could rent a horse on the beach. Like something out of a Conan comic strip, the large, muscled Craig Monson would ride a white horse while looking like a medieval conqueror on the central Eurasian steppe.

Intellectually curious about the world and different cultures, particularly after spending much of his late adolescence confined to a steel cell, Craig would take the time to absorb the smaller nuances of this "cultural exchange." For instance, on one occasion, they were driving back to the border when Craig noticed some unorthodox houses alongside the road.

The hulking bodybuilder knocked on the door of a stranger's home to kindly ask a Mexican woman whether he could look inside her home. There was nothing illicit or conniving about his request; he just wanted to see how she lived. After Craig offered $20 as a payment of good faith, the woman and her kids took him through their modest residence. Craig noticed that the floor had an unusual dark color to it. When he asked about it, the woman explained that it was made from mud mixed with pig's blood. For a man whose life had revolved around his neighborhood and prolonged stays in various correctional facilities, this out of the ordinary addition to a "floor plan" blew Craig's mind.

The entertainment, the performance, and the degrees of culture from these trips stayed with Craig. Similarly, a comparable type of lasting impression was imprinted upon the memories of those who witnessed Craig's training routine during those days.

In fact, many iron enthusiasts associate Big Craig Monson with the regular strength shows he put on for awestruck crowds at the fabled pit of Venice's Muscle Beach. But the history connecting Craig to this mecca of muscle is complex. Monson, along with his lifelong friend and training partner Donnie Boy, first arrived at Venice Beach in 1966. At 16 years old, already enamored with all things strength related, Craig wanted to get at those rows of weights, gleaming under the idyllic California sun. Although a long way from his birthplace in the racially divided South, Craig still encountered racism in that story-book land of California. The gatekeeper at the pit refused to take their money. Never one to let obstacles stand in the way of his strength-gaining quest, Craig, along with Donnie Boy, started to hop the fence surrounding the gym. Over and over, they did this. It became clear that these abnormally muscled teens were going to get to train, one way or another. So they finally accepted a teenage Monson's money, begrudgingly.

The scenario was much different 10 years later, in 1976, when Craig returned to the gym at Venice. The pit was run by a guy named B.J., who was just out of the pen himself. With that in common, along with a sincere commitment to the iron, Craig started to make regular trips to Muscle Beach on the weekends, when he would work out with B.J., Big Bill Pettis, and Big West (who was one of the strongest dudes in the pit, with a 630-pound bench press). Craig would show up in the morning with a gym bag filled with his lifting gear and pack-ages of turkey and fruit, which he would eat between sets. And during those sets, he put on a show, a performance, a strength spectacle still talked about today.

He also made connections with legendary men of strength. As anyone who watched pro wrestling during the 1980s remembers, Hulk Hogan would often reference Venice Beach and the muscle-building platform there. Monson fondly remembers lifting with Hogan and then sharing a bottle of Ripple (i.e., the White Claw of the late 1970s) after the training session.

Known by many for his work in gritty crime movies like *Blood In, Blood Out* and *Heat* and known to even more because of the cult classic film *Machete*, Danny Trejo is that rare Hollywood specimen. He is authentic. Like Craig, Trejo was a product of the penal system.

Introduced to drugs at a young age by his uncle, Trejo was in and out of jail for over a decade until he broke his cycle of recidivism. Danny became sober through a 12-step program while serving time at the infamous San Quentin Prison, where he was the reigning lightweight and welterweight boxing champion (the same uncle who turned him onto drugs also taught him to box). Once released, Trejo made a commitment to turn his life around by following a firm but simple philosophy of helping others. Interestingly, Danny found that the more he helped others, the better his life became.

While working as a drug counselor for some people connected to the movie business, Trejo got his break into show business. A fellow inmate from his days at San Quentin, Edward Bunker had become a prominent writer, and he remembered that Danny had some hands. So, Bunker brought in Danny to teach actor Eric Roberts how to box for the film *Runaway Train*. The film's director saw quickly that Trejo had "the look" and gave him a small part, to add authenticity to the movie. That was the beginning of his storied movie career.

In 1979, Danny and Craig were ex-cons who liked to train at Venice—Danny the former pugilist looking to stay sharp and Craig the aspiring bodybuilder. Along with an affinity for working out, the two men shared a perspective on the human condition only understood by those who refused to let their time behind bars destroy their core humanity. Sadly, many leave incarceration battered, broken, and bitter. But both Danny and Craig share an almost infectious and interminable positivity. Perhaps this sentiment, more than anything else, ignited the spark of their enduring friendship.

Danny trusted Craig implicitly. Through the 1980s, Danny would often leave his son with Craig at Venice. While enjoying his post-workout pump from his training sessions at the Pit, Craig would babysit Danny's kid (with a little red wagon) in the sandbox at Venice Beach. Now known as an international star, during Craig's bodybuilding career, Danny would regularly show up in the wings to support his friend. Still today, the famous actor and retired bodybuilder will often catch up over a steak at the Pantry in downtown Los Angeles (one of Craig's favorite restaurants).

As mythic as the strength show was at Venice, City Gym remained Craig's primary facility during this period, and Craig fell into the almost monastic, monotonous routine required for any human who dreams of superhuman achievements. After their regular sessions at City Gym, Monson and his workout partners would feed (they did more than just eat) at the iconic Pantry, ordering a butterflied beef steak tenderloin. Both the training and the regular trips to the Pantry fueled Monson for his blossoming bodybuilding career.

In the world of bodybuilding, conversations often turn to the topic of steroids. Perhaps rightly so, considering the way in which many current bodybuilders look more bloated than dense, inflated than sturdy, and processed than powerful.

When you look at the old photos of Craig from his competitive days, you see an image of symmetrical muscularity and unquestionable power. It is the look, or build, cultivated only by years of high-volume training. When it comes to steroids and performance enhancers, Monson is candid on his history with those tools. He used them to refine his already developed physique, in the same way a mechanic may use a specific tool to fine-tune particular machinery under the hood of an elite sports car.

Craig did not build his body with steroids; he used particular items to refine what was already developed through hard work.

As deep as Monson was in the iron game, his introduction to steroids came relatively late. Craig's first bodybuilding show was Mr. Los Angeles in 1979. At the time, Craig followed a somewhat crude method for getting cut-up before the competition. He would take a predigested protein (found on the shelves at Ralph's supermarket) along with lots of strawberries and pineapple. He would also mix tuna (with the spring water poured out) with half a cup of warm water and some lemon juice in a blender. The concoction was so daunting that Craig would hold his nose just to get it down.

But when he got backstage at Mr. Los Angeles with Rory Leidelmeyer (who would go on to win the event), Craig unabashedly asked how he got so big while keeping his definition.

To which Rory responded with candor: "Well, big man, when you changed your cycle, what did you change? What cycle did you use to get cut?"

Craig was perplexed.

"My cycle?" he asked in confusion. "I'm using tuna and store-bought protein packets."

Unabated, Rory was more direct in his explanation: "No, what did you change with your drugs?"

"Man, I don't know anything about drugs. I'm not taking any of that," Craig responded in shock.

As much as Craig had seen on the streets, behind bars, and in gyms, he was still somewhat naïve to some things. He had suspected folks were using some kind of performance enhancers at the pit in Venice, but he didn't know much about them.

Craig's introduction to steroids came in 1982, while he was training at Iron Man's Gym in downtown Los Angeles. Unsurprisingly, Craig quickly established himself as the big man at the gym, and as such, it was common for gym regulars and employees to attempt to endear themselves to him. One such interaction took place with this guy from Belize named Julio, who worked the front desk of the gym.

Craig would drive over to the gym from Hollywood and get changed for his training session. When he came out, Julio made it a habit to have a small bag of "vitamins" waiting for him. Now, the packaging resembled the multivitamins sold at 7-Eleven and other such convenience stores, so Craig thought nothing of it.

This exchange became routine.

Julio would say, "Here you go, Big Craig." Then he would rip open the bag and pour a couple blue pills and a small white pill into a protein drink.

Well, Craig started to notice some things during his workout sessions. On one day in particular, he was hitting bench. He banged out 405 a couple of times, real smooth. He told his training partner, Big Willie, "Give another quarter [25 pounds]."

Instead, they put on a plate. Now there was 495 on the bar. But Craig was so jacked up he didn't seem to care. He got under it and banged out 10 reps.

His lifting partners started laughing.

"What's so funny?" he asked.

"Big Craig," they said, "you just hit five plates for ten."

Craig had never done that before. He looked in the mirror and saw the plates still spinning from the ride. Then he noticed a vein, a thick vein, as thick as his finger, coming down from his hair to his eyebrow.

Craig yelled, "Yo Julio! What are you giving me?!"

Julio came running over, "Monson, let me talk to you."

It turned out Julio was giving Craig Dianabol and Anadrol-50. To ease some of Monson's uncertainty, Julio invited Craig to see his doctor over at Cedars-Sinai, named Walter J. Cox.

At the visit, Dr. Cox took one look at Craig and saw a potential gold mine. Dr. Cox quickly filled Julio's prescription, then he turned to Craig and said, "I need to talk with you."

They walked into his office. After closing the door, the doctor turned to Monson and said, "I'm going to use you as my publicity. You will be my foot soldier, and I will give you everything you need."

"What do you mean?" asked Craig.

"Let's put it this way. What do you weigh?"

"My weight? Oh, I weigh about 255."

"I'm going to take you to 300 pounds."

That's the day Craig met Dr. Frankenstein.

Of course, Monson was not the only bodybuilder working with Dr. Cox. The outside of the doctor's office was like a reunion—all the top bodybuilders would be sitting there, waiting for their turn with the doctor.

Dr. Cox made sure to have bodybuilders behind the desk, as well. Two bodybuilders, with 20-inch arms that filled out their white smocks, sent a message that this office knew the score. The bodybuilders were in the hands of folks who knew the intricacies of competitive bodybuilding.

Before that transformational experience, Craig's first show was the Mr. Los Angeles event. After that, he did a novice event in Oceanside (also in 1979). Later, Monson was the feature attraction in a number of small, local shows, before reaching a national audience with Mr. America (in 1984, held in Pasadena) and Mr. USA (held at the Sands Hotel in Las Vegas), along with an international audience with the Night of the Crystal in London and the 1983 Mr. World in Geneva, Switzerland. Monson's final show would be the Orange County Classic in 1985.

Along with these more formal shows, Craig did some guest posing appearances at the Palm Spring Classic, The Battle of the Gladiators, and Mr. Arizona. Craig also did an event at the California Institute for Men correctional facility in Chino, where he did a posing show as part of a larger program which was organized with the intent of raising the morale of the inmates. Monson was following Arnold Schwarzenegger, who did a series of exhibitions at Chino before him. Yet, unlike the Arnold, Craig, of course, was formerly a resident of the California penal system. So, as amazing and legendary as Schwarzenegger was, and is, with Craig, prisoners received a more poignant message: With strength, you can transform your life. Even in this brief window of time, Big Monson left a deep and lasting imprint in the memories of fans of muscle.

The British physicist Isaac Newton said, "If I have seen further, it is by standing on the shoulders of giants." For all of Monson's massive strength, he is strengthened by his friendships, training partners, and mentors. Although he never had a formal coach, from 1979 through 1980, a doctor named Finny would help to guide Craig's training and serve as an aide during competition preparation. Finny took Craig to his novice show in Oceanside, which he won. However, on the drive back from the event, Finny started in on how all of the other competitors were close to winning, within striking distance.

Then as now, Craig is neither a narcissist nor a braggart. For a man who has walked some of the roughest prison yards and revealed his bare body to thousands of adoring fans, Craig harbors no illusions about himself. In his presence, you feel a powerful confidence, but a cocky ego is unmistakably missing. Craig is also perceptive. He reads the energy of those around him and is cautious about whom he lets come close. So, when Finny starting talking about how great everyone else on stage looked, Craig distanced himself from him. He did this not out of arrogance or haughtiness, but rather out of a need to guard himself.

As Craig learned from Geronimo Pratt during their time at San Quentin, be careful about whom you let in your inner circle (both physical and emotional). This is true for everyday folks, and it is even more relevant for those among us who make the decision to pursue excellence.

Perhaps the tendency to keep people at a distance is the reason Craig never had a long-term coach. More likely, Monson never found a mentor with the character to channel his strength. Nevertheless, Craig was close to many of the greats from the golden age of bodybuilding. He stood shoulder to shoulder with legends like Sergio Oliva and Arnold Schwarzenegger.

It seems that we live in a time when many folks are quick to speak and slow to listen. Learning opportunities pass many by because their mouths are open and their ears are closed, when the opposite should be the case. To this point, Jimi Hendrix is rumored to have realized that "knowledge speaks, but wisdom listens."

Craig had the wisdom to listen to the knowledge of Oliva when he passed along training tips. A firm believer in fully developing your lats, Oliva told him to do behind the neck pull-ups every day. He also preached the importance of push-ups to keep a full chest. Oliva was known for a lean waist, which he developed with a simple but effective movement. Rather than doing side bends with weights (which he did not like because they would "wake up," or muscularly develop, the oblique muscles and make the waist look big), Sergio used a long stick placed lightly upon the back of his neck. With his arms draped over the ends, Oliva would do side bends with the stick to keep his waist tight and small.

More generally, Oliva was a firm believer in heavy weight. Or, as he told Craig: "Maximum poundage will build mass that will last!"

That means don't skimp on the iron. Pile the weight on the bar.

Monson also listened to the little tips passed along from Schwarzenegger, who told him to train his calves and forearms every day. Now, there are those who would say that this would be overtraining. However, people who have taken a class on the topics of physiology, kinesiology, and sports medicine, or all of us who have been in the trenches of hard training, know that smaller muscles recover more quickly than large muscles. During one day when Schwarzenegger and Monson were benching together at Venice Beach, Arnold also passed along more personalized advice to Craig. He suggested that Craig was hindering himself on the bench because of his close hand placement. With Craig's broad shoulders, Arnold recommended he use a wider grip. Receptive to knowledge from wise sources, Craig started to go "collar to collar" with his grip and found that the weight would go straight up.

It's not enough to just surround yourself with strength. You must be willing to open yourself to those rare learning moments. The humility required to receive and implement advice from fellow men of strength made Craig even stronger.

THE WORKOUT

Back in the days of Reg Park, Sergio Olivia, and Arnold Schwarzenegger, procuring serious strength was a foregone conclusion for any serious bodybuilding regimen. Men of muscle trained to become men of strength.

What the hell happened?

Steroids and other performance enhancers became not just commonplace, but changed from being a tool to help bodybuilders bust through plateaus to a crutch for those who started taking steroids as teenagers and refused to train without them!

In this environment of artificially pumped-up lifters who lacked discipline and approached the iron game with the lack of sincerity expected from those who prolong their adolescent ways to the point of absurdity, Craig was a breath of fresh air. He was a throwback to the era of the founding fathers of bodybuilding, who regularly performed feats of strength alongside their posing routines. Craig's physique was a Michelangelo-like portrait, painted with a brush of heavy-ass pig iron and more volume done in one session than most muscle-building enthusiasts do in a whole month.

Some of Craig's feats of strength included the following (all weights in pounds):

- Bench Press 585 x 5 Reps
- Bench Press 405 x 24 Reps (4 Sets)
- Bench Press 315 x 50 Reps (4 Sets)
- Dumbbell Bench Press 200 (Each Hand) x 10 Reps
- Straight-Arm Dumbbell Flys 100 (Each Hand) x 8 Reps
- Cross-Over Dumbbell Curls 150 (Each Hand) x 8 Reps
- Dumbbell Curls 115 (Each Hand) x 8 Reps
- Deadlift 500 x 5 Reps (Only Time Ever Deadlifting)
- Bicep Barbell Curls 275 x 5 Reps
- Walking Lunges 315 x 20 Yards
- Front Squats 405 x 4 Reps
- Skull Crushers 315 x 12 Reps

Craig performed these feats up until his fifties, and even today, at 70 years old, he is built like a brick shithouse. Craig always heeded the wisdom of Sergio Oliva. Craig remembers a conversation they shared backstage at a bodybuilding show, when Sergio said that when you train heavy, you build "the mass that lasts." A believer in aesthetic muscularity and functional strength, Sergio was a Cuban champion in weightlifting long before he considered throwing on the posing trunks.

While not a competitive weightlifter, Craig needed strength as a youngster to be the undisputed alpha male of the LA streets, where he reigned supreme from Watts to Compton to Beverly Hills.

In the Crowbar Hotel (a.k.a. "prison"), Craig carried on his legacy by becoming the permanent yard hog. Inside, Craig was not one to rest on his laurels; every day he put his title on the line and viewed himself as a champion ready to take all comers. But, like Rocky Marciano, Craig was never defeated.

As bodybuilding became more popular, well-to-do suburban white kids from all over the United States headed west and began to train at the idyllic environment of Muscle Beach in Venice Beach, California. Living this dream was often on their parents' dime; these kids, often in their teenage years and not knowing the true value of years of hard work, wolfed down steroids.

Sure, the results came fast. However, they were built with a faulty foundation; they had no real strength base. So the results dissipated just as quickly. It was not uncommon to see the physique of a pumped-up 21-year-old on a cycle rapidly deteriorate into a body that resembled the 1980s cult actor Pee-Wee Herman once the cycle ended.

Craig did not start using steroids until his mid-thirties. With the decades of hard, natural training, Craig had created a synergistic anabolic storm that resulted in the development of a Schwarzenegger-like chest, 23-inch arms cold, and a tiny, tapered waist measuring a mere 30 inches at 6-foot-2, 270 pounds.

As a competitor, Craig was fueled daily by a local Korean BBQ restaurant. The restaurant adored Craig and would change seasonings, meats, and preparation style depending on whether the goal was off-season mass building or fat loss for contest prep.

Craig also credits his training partners for his success as a bodybuilder. These included both Big Frank and Big Willie. The last names of both of these iron gladiators remain unknown. But, in that time, in that training environment, surnames took a back seat to the mentality you brought to training. The mindset was one that had a striking resemblance to the warrior monks of ancient times. Craig's was an anabolic journey that came at the cost of a normal social life, imbibing in wine, chasing women, and reveling in song.

Craig was like a monk, a monk of the iron.

Craig's Success

As a competitive bodybuilder, Craig won plenty of contests. However, in reality, Craig was an Olympia-level competitor.

Why did Craig never compete on this level?

Michael Christian never won the Olympia, but he definitely should have. While Christian played the "Joe Weider game" to a point, he still went out, posed in a do-rag, and was a Crip; in our estimation, Joe Weider and the bodybuilding establishment felt that White America (bodybuilding's primary fan base) could not handle Christian.

Contrast that to Craig Monson.

Monson was invited numerous times by Weider to train at Gold's Gym with all of Weider's guys, but Craig just never liked the vibe at the place. Monson would show up to train hard and heavy, only to be advised by other bodybuilders "this was no longer needed." With modern chemistry, the new way was pump up a little bit, then socialize with the aerobics bunnies. By the 1980s, bodybuilders would even color coordinate their workout attire so they could pose for Weider and company post workout.

Basically, Gold's had become a brownnosing fest for Weider. Bodybuilders there wanted fame, notoriety, and whatever financial peanuts Weider might throw at them.

Craig was about the go, not the show.

If every last person on Earth died, the Iron Monk, Craig Monson, would be training heavy and pumping in complete solitude. Craig cared more about the journey than the destination!

At nationals one year, the legendary John Grimek told Craig he was light-years ahead of every other competitor; the fans agreed and booed the eventual winner on stage, who privately conceded to Craig that Craig was the real winner that night.

At the end of the day, Craig never won major professional titles because he would not sacrifice his iron soul or his journey to play someone else's game. And if Craig had to do it all over, he would not change a damn thing!

Let's look at Craig's favorite training split as a professional bodybuilder. Oftentimes, these training sessions lasted over three hours, but nothing ever got in the way of Craig's training.

Monday (Day 1)/Friday (Day 5)

Exercise	Sets	Reps	Weight	Rest Interval
Push-Ups against the Wall	3	25-30	Bodyweight	60 sec
Bench Press	8	8-12	Heavy as possible	120 sec
Incline Bench Press	8	8-12	Heavy as possible	120 sec
Flat Dumbbell Bench Press	4-6	6-8	Heavy as possible	60 sec
Incline Dumbbell Bench Press	4-5	8-10	Light	60 sec
Dumbbell Fly Massive Stretches	4	8-10	Moderate	60 sec
Most Muscular Cable Flys	4	15-20	Moderate	90 sec

Continue

Exercise	Sets	Reps	Weight	Rest Interval
Wide-Grip Pulldowns behind Neck	4	20	Heavy	60 sec
Wide-Grip Pulldowns	4	15	Heavy	60 sec
Lean-Back Lat Pulldowns	4	8-10	Moderate	60 sec
T-Bar Prison Rows	4	15-20	Moderate	60 sec
One-Arm Dumbbell Rows	3	12-15	Moderate	60 sec
Seated Cable Rows	4	6-10	Heavy	60 sec
Stretch Bent-Over Rows	4	20-25	Light	60 sec
Push-Ups	1	Max	Bodyweight	

Special Notes

Push-Ups against the Wall: These are done just to get a slight pump and blood flow; fatigue is not the goal.

Bench Press: Go as heavy as possible. The first two sets are warm-up sets.

Incline Bench Press: Go as heavy as possible. The first two sets are warm-up sets.

Flat Dumbbell Bench Press: Go as heavy as possible. The first set is a warm-up set.

Incline Dumbbell Bench Press: Go as heavy as possible. The first set is a warm-up set.

Dumbbell Fly Massive Stretches: These have been described already; now Craig would include a max-reps set with 30 pounds less than he was using for each set.

Most Muscular Cable Flys: Craig now had cables, so he would simply perform a most muscular pose using cables as resistance.

His last two sets, after hitting failure, he would include two additional drop sets (so each of the last two sets is really like three each); each drop would be approximately 30 percent, so if Craig was using 100 pounds, he would drop to 70 first then 45.

Wide-Grip Pulldowns behind Neck: These were performed behind the neck, with the full stack and whatever plates Craig could fit on. Each set, Craig would do at least five forced reps with a training partner's assistance.

Wide-Grip Pulldowns: Using the same weight he used behind the neck, Craig would execute these to the front side, minus the forced reps.

Lean-Back Lat Pulldowns: Similar to the feeling of a sternum pull-up, Craig really focused on squeezing his rhomboids, making this movement almost like a hybrid vertical pull/rowing movement.

T-Bar Prison Rows were performed with moderate weight, with the focus being on contraction of the upper-back muscles, not bar weight. Craig would place the end of an empty barbell into the corner of a room, then rest a heavy dumbbell or some weight plates on it to hold it down. He would load the opposite end of the bar with plates and straddle it. He would bend over at the hips until his torso was at about a 45-degree angle to the floor with his arms extended. He used a V-grip handle (the kind you see at a cable station) under the bar, and he held with both hands. From here, keeping his lower back in its natural arch, he squeezed his shoulder blades together and pulled the bar until the plates touched his chest. Craig was worried about his lower back, so he never maxed the weight on these, but he routinely hit 15+ reps with five plates.

One-Arm Dumbbell Rows: Craig's opposing hand and knee were on the opposing side contrasted to his work side, using strict form.

Seated Cable Rows: These were normal seated rows with a V-handle. Craig would go very heavy on these, and his final two sets consisted of two triple drop sets!

Stretch Bent-Over Rows: Like a normal bent-over row, except Craig stood up on the end of the bench press. This was not a party trick but helped Craig extend his range of motion by not being stopped by the floor. This loaded stretch provided Craig with a hellacious overload.

Push-Ups: Even at over 270 pounds, at the end of all this, Craig would routinely bang out 100+ reps straight.

Tuesday (Day 2)/Thursday (Day 4)

Exercise	Sets	Reps	Weight	Rest Interval
Curls	1	25	100	
Triceps Extensions	5	8-12	Heavy	None
Straight Bar Curls (Supersetted Triceps Extension)		8-12	Heavy	
Three-Quarter Curls	4		See Description	90 sec
Dumbbell 21 Curls	4	7-7-7	Heavy	120 sec
Barbell 21 Curls	4	7-7-7	Heavy	75 Sec
Dumbbell Extensions Behind the Head	4-6	8-12	Moderate	60 sec
Overhead Press	4-6	10-12	Heavy	120 sec

Curls: Craig always used a straight bar because that is all he had; the straight bar, however, forced his arms to remain in supination, forcing his biceps to work overtime. 100 pounds was a warm-up weight for Craig.

Triceps Extensions/Straight Bar Curls: These were performed in a superset style, back and forth. The only rest was spotting a partner on triceps extensions. One man was curling, one man was doing triceps extensions, one man was spotting. Everything was in close quarters to minimize rest periods.

Three-Quarter Curls: See earlier explanation.

Dumbbell 21 Curls: Executed for seven reps of each of the following movements, without dropping the dumbbells. First, alternating dumbbell crossover curls to the chin, next traditional dumbbell curls, and finish with hammer curls, while consciously flexing the triceps on the negative.

Barbell 21 Curls: With a straight bar, Craig would curl the first seven reps, from the bottom of the movement up to the halfway point. For the next seven reps, he would do the top half of the movement. Then, Craig finished with seven full reps.

Dumbbell Extensions behind the Head with the concentration curls. After raising the dumbbell above his head until his arms were fully extended, Craig would slowly lower the weight, grabbing it by the end of the bell, back behind his head; really focusing on the stretch, he would do the movement stretching to the right side of his head and then to the left in an alternating fashion.

Overhead Press: Craig would alternate these between seated and standing overhead presses. Seated hammered the muscle better, but standing helped work the entire body and keep the raw functional strength. Craig did not need more shoulder work because of all of his pressing work; he would, however, periodically sprinkle in lateral raises throughout the week.

Wednesday

At this point in Craig's career, he knew he needed a serious set of wheels to match his consummate upper-body development. Not one to back down from a challenge, he grabbed the bull by the balls and twisted those sons of bitches off with beautiful leg development. Initially, this started with Craig pushing his car up the hill at the Griffith Park Observatory, and it evolved into a more traditional, but still rugged, leg day.

Exercise	Sets	Reps	Weight	Rest Interval
Front Squats	4	12-20	Heavy	120 sec
Walking Lunges	4	10 yards	Heavy	120 sec
Hack Squats	4	8-12	Heavy	90 sec
Leg Press	4	10-15	Heavy	90 sec
Leg Extensions	5	25	Moderate	60 sec
Leg Curls	5	15-20	Moderate	60 sec

Front Squats: Done with a deep, full range of motion, Craig often did reps with 405. Craig preferred these to back squats because of his lower-back injury attained repping 500 pounds on deadlifts.

Walking Lunges: These were done for distance so Craig could get a huge stretch; fewer reps was better (making sure his knee never touched the ground). Craig did these with 315 and felt they really helped build the glute/ham tie. Since then, they have become a staple of Ronnie Coleman and many other well-developed bodybuilders who are willing to put in the work.

Hack Squats: Craig would go deep on these and do them in a continuous tension style.

Leg Press: Craig could cut loose on these without having to think about his lower back, working up to over 1600 pounds.

Leg Extensions: High reps were the name of the game here, heeding the advice of Tom Platz, who was famous for his uncanny leg development.

Leg Curls: Craig did these heavy as possible but 100 percent strict.

Thursday
Monday's workout BUT higher reps and lighter weight.

Friday

Tuesday's workout BUT higher reps and lighter weight. However, if Craig felt really excited or enthusiastic this day, by feel, it would morph into a heavy one.

Saturday

Off

Sunday

Show-off day. This day, Craig would show off his multiple feats of strength at the Pit on Venice Beach (not the color-coordinated Gold's Gym).

Miscellaneous

Arnold told Craig to work calves every day, so he did! Craig got the most out of the donkey calf raise. He also worked his forearms and abdominals daily.

Final Thoughts

In part three of the *Rocky* movie series/manual for life, Rocky Balboa lost the "eye of the tiger." So, he has to return to a no-nonsense, no-frills type of training. He ditches the plush circle jerk masquerading as a gym and goes back to the basics by training at the rough-and-tumble gym of Apollo Creed's early days.

In a similar type of no-nonsense, no-frills environment, Monson made his best gains in the hard-core gyms like City Gym, the prison yard, and Hollywood Gym.

As a competitive bodybuilder, the iron monk, Craig Monson, experienced huge success, but he never gave an inch to corporate America; like Frank Sinatra, Craig did it his way.

Chapter Four

THE STORY

Held on July 4, 1939, the inaugural Mr. America show crowned its first winner, named "America's Best Built Man." Although the event was started by the Amateur Athletic Union (AAU), Joe and Ben Weider's International Federation of Bodybuilding and Fitness (IFBB) held a rival contest from 1959 until 1977. With both organizations vying for the recognition to hold the competition and a myriad of muscled competitors striving for the coveted title, Mr. America became a sought-after name.

In 1984, the AAU Mr. America was held in Pasadena, and the massive presence of Big Craig Monson filled the stage, awed the audience, and left an impact on the legendary event. The pictures that captured the evening show Monson in peak form. Broad, symmetrical, and vascular, it was clearly Craig's night. But the judges didn't see it that way.

One of the judges was Dr. Walter J. Cox, who served as Craig's sports doctor, and he gave it to him straight. During prejudging, Dr. Cox told Monson that it was clearly his night. But "the table" was against him. The other judges didn't want him to win. So, the title eluded Craig.

The casual observer and keen critic of bodybuilding, alike, knew that Craig was the winner.

Craig's clear dominance began even before the show. He took all of the preparatory measures to look his best—niacin pills and a few nips of Manischewitz wine in a sliver flask for vascularity. Craig was pumped and primed for victory. The eventual winner of the 1984 Mr. America event, Arthur Prince, and Monson were sharing the warm-up area. Right away, Craig could see the striking difference between himself and Prince. By his own description, Craig's build was like "an oak tree, crackly and hard." In contrast, Arthur Prince's body lacked physical maturity. It was "baby smooth, like a clean sidewalk."

The discrepancy in their maturity was also displayed in how they carried themselves during the warm-up. Just like back in the pen, Craig was a hog. He started calling shots. In a jovial fashion, he would chide Arthur Prince, calling out to him, "Where you going junior, get back over here!"

When they shared the stage, Craig stridently took the center of the stage, where the light was. He took his place next to Prince to hit his poses. Arthur walked away. Monson had the stage, light, and attention to himself.

But the Boston native Arthur Prince had four judges from Boston tipping the scales in his favor.

Even the DJ was conspiring against Craig. In the middle of Craig's routine, the DJ cut his posing music. Not skipping a beat, Craig, a veteran of street gang violence and prison yard politics, picked the DJ up by his neck, and a general commotion erupted.

After the show, a number of well-wishers gathered around a dejected Craig and offered words of encouragement, consolation, and reassurance. One old-timer, leaning heavily on a cane, hung back until the crowd thinned. After a number of spectators had their moment with Craig, the old guy shuffled forward.

He put both his hands on Craig's shoulders and looked him straight in the eye.

"Tonight was your night." The stranger's voice echoed with surprising volume and strength. "You should have won tonight. Don't forget that. Tonight, you could have won Mr. Olympia," he said. With that, he walked off.

Clearly moved by the words, Craig was still processing the experience when somebody in his entourage turned to him.

"Do you know who that was?"

"No," Craig said in candor and confusion.

"That was John Grimek."

Now, everyone in the audience and anyone looking back at the images from that night can see easily that it was, indeed, Craig's show. Sadly, not getting a fair shake at the 1984 Mr. America broke Craig's spirit. And, as any experienced therapist or astute viewer of life experiences will tell you, there is no quick fix, easy cure, or magic pill to remedy that.

The spirit housed in Craig's mountain of muscle became dormant, and Monson walked away from competitive bodybuilding.

The great Greek thinker Aristotle said, "Man is a goal-seeking animal. His life only has meaning if he is reaching out and striving for his goals." Monson had scraped tooth and nail to get his life in order after completing his time inside of the California penal system, and his dreams of bodybuilding glory filled his life with purpose, direction, and meaning.

However, his dream bubble burst on that night in Pasadena. Of course, Craig was familiar with the experience of inequity. Fleeing seething racism as a child, raised in the inner city, and convicted of the "crime" of killing a home intruder, Craig had encountered unfairness, injustice, and blatant bias. But this was different.

They had taken his dream, his goal. Craig had done everything right. He had paid his dues and put in the time. They still took it.

The iron game was his magnetic north, and without that compass point, Craig was lost. This is a common predicament in the human condition; as the philosopher Friedrich Nietzsche wrote, "By losing your goal, you have lost your way."

Now, Craig was adrift. He was going to have to find some grounding. But that can require time, effort, and planning. In the meanwhile, his life trajectory got a little off course.

In that sad but reappearing cliché, Craig began to party. Up and down the clubs of Hollywood, Big Monson emerged as a regular sight, drinking, dancing, and engaging in general debauchery. As one night floated into another, Craig's trips to the gym became less frequent. He eventually found that an evening party continued into the next day, until the party didn't stop.

The stoic lifestyle had served Craig. He did not see the cans of sardines, the long hours in the gym, and the shunning of hedonistic pursuits as a drab existence. He built a body like a classic Renaissance sculpture carved from a slab of marble. He followed a routine that provided a sense of emotional equilibrium, gave him a clear direction, and filled his life with a sense of purpose.

There are many who perceive the monotonous program of hard training and clean living as some sort of imprisonment. Well, Craig had been to prison. He spent time in some of the darkest, dingiest, and most depressing correctional facilities. And he found that his mindset and his routine were all that he could control in that environment. By controlling both, Craig found a liberating strength in his psychological and physical enhancement.

It's been said that the hardest prison to escape is your mind. Through rigorous training, a disciplined diet, and complete commitment to his program, Craig shook off the shackles of confinement. He found emancipation, and, perhaps, brief glimpses of enlightenment.

Ironically, once he was no longer bound to his training program, Craig found himself in the deep crevices of confinement. He had become an addict. Substances that were foreign to him during the time of his hard training became a false beacon of hope, an unreliable cloak of protection against the harsh reality of a life without direction, goals, and purpose.

Craig knew he needed help and he headed for recovery, finding a place in the mountains of Santa Clarita. The rehab center offered 12 meetings a day, where Monson heard the stories of those who had fallen into the same trap of addiction. He started to meditate and found a sense of grounding.

Craig also found that he was by no means anonymous. At the rehab center, there was an old-time member of the notorious prison gang the Black Guerilla Family, also known as the BGF, who had written the gang's constitution. As a veteran of the California penal system, he had heard about the legend of Craig Monson. Similarly, many others at the rehab center had heard the stories, some fantastic and some more believable, about Big Craig.

Craig grew up on the streets of LA. In that environment, your reputation is your most prized possession. You work for it and defend it fiercely. It was life-affirming to hear that his reputation stretched across time and place.

Some of Craig's family wanted this kind of coveted street reputation, and they pursued that status inside of the treacherous world of street gangs.

Originally a small movement from Craig's old neighborhood, by the late 1980s and into the early 1990s, the Crip street gangs evolved into a massive monster of many different subgroups, or sets. One such Crip set is known as the 87 Kitchen Crips, a name taken from the Kitchen Liquor store on the corner of Florence and 87th streets where the clique was initially formed.

Now, inside of each set, certain gang members rose to prominence and recognition as OGs, or original gangsters. This was a proud badge and a source of esteem in many inner-city Los Angeles neighborhoods. An early member of the 87 Kitchen Crips, Craig's younger brother, James "Big Psycho Runt" Stewart, pursued that status with an unabashed zeal and unyielding conviction.

Hearing that his brother was involved in gangs was nothing new or necessarily surprising for Craig. Involvement with the coarse life of the streets was a reality in Craig's neighborhood. But, when Craig heard his brother's criminal behavior was increasing in scope, frequency, and severity, he felt a fraternal obligation to step in.

In a conversation eerily similar to the warning Craig offered to Tookie, Craig tried to warn his brother about the dangers of gang violence. Yet, like with Tookie, his brother would not take the advice. Sadly, he became a victim of strife on the streets of LA.

Unsurprisingly, the loss of a family member, the battles with addiction, and the absence of bodybuilding in his life made this a tough time for Craig.

To restore a sense of balance in his life, Craig needed to find his way back to training, to the iron, to the weights. His journey back to lifting unfolded gradually and organically.

In the mid-1990s, Craig was running a large linen warehouse in the Los Angeles Valley, on Sherman Way. During this time, his body started to yearn for the euphoria brought on by a good workout. Listening to his body, and perhaps something deeper in his soul, Craig started to move around a little. He brought some dumbbells into the warehouse, and during his downtime, Craig would find a corner of solitude. Alone, in the corner of a large commercial warehouse, Craig started banging out push-ups and moving those dumbbells to train his arms.

His body started to awaken.

This was far from a triumphant return to the iron. This was a temperate turn to the relationship which served Craig throughout his life and informed his sense of self.

Now, every day on his drive home, he would pass by a gym, one in particular. The gym was called Hollywood Gym, and on some base, foundational, unconscious level, it seemed to be calling out to Big Craig.

So, one day in 1996, Craig finally decided to stop and check it out. It had been a long time since the great Craig Monson had set foot in an iron pit. But the clink of the weights, the smell of the chalk, and the audible strain of lifters brought back a flood of memories and a connection to his childhood fascination of all things strength.

He signed up and started to show up, to lift again. When he first came back, he shunned the flashy spandex, sweat suits, and workout outfits. Instead, he favored training with a big denim jacket, in the style of the old prison days. To a certain extent, this was a nod to his time in the penitentiary. More than that, Craig was self-conscious, insecure.

The time away from the weights and the struggle with addiction had left his body looking like a shell of its former self. The memories and photos of Big Craig in his prime capturing and keeping the attention of an awestruck crowd were no longer his reality. He stopped going to Venice because he didn't want to keep answering the same question: "What happened to Big Craig?"

But, a hog is still a hog. Craig was back at the gym hitting the weights, looking around, seeing who was the big dog at the gym. It was quickly evident that it was a dude named Big Pete, out of Chicago. Craig watched him, and Big Pete watched him right back.

One day, the silence was broken.

"Hey," Big Pete said to Craig, "you look like that big old dude from the '80s, what was his name? Something Monson?"

"Craig Monson."

"Yeah, that's it! You've heard that you look like him?"

"Look like him? I am him. I am Craig Monson!"

At that, a kinship was struck, and Big Pete asked Craig to spot him on the bench press; he was going for 315 for six. Big Pete came up from the set all pumped with pride and lactic acid.

Monson, still a hog, felt something start to waken up deep inside of him.

"Pete," Craig spoke up, "give me a month."

"A month? A month for what?"

"One month and I'll show you how to move that weight."

Pete just laughed it off, good-naturedly. You see, at that time, Craig was only working out with the bar on the bench press.

Nonetheless, Monson remained adamant about his statement.

"One month," Craig reiterated.

In the meantime, Big Pete, who was the head bouncer at a Hollywood nightclub called Dublin's, got Monson a job working security at the bar.

This meant that Craig would be back in the public eye, potentially running into some folks who would remember Big Monson from the old days. So, Craig stayed "undercover," as he put it. While working, he wore an oversized security sweatshirt (5XL) to hide the state of his build. Keeping a low profile did not stop Craig from appreciating the new gig. The comradery with the other bouncers was nice; the rib eye steaks (Craig's preferred cut) he got for free from the kitchen were even nicer.

One month later, the entire bouncing staff (all 16 of them) and the owner of Dublin's piled into Hollywood Gym to watch Craig's bench show. He piled the three plates on each side, got under the bar, and, like a craftsman returning to his trade, found his old grip, going "collar to collar."

Before the lift, Craig looked up at his gathered audience.

"I'm going to show ya'll something."

With that, he hoisted the bar and went to work. As he banged out the reps, the bouncers shouted out the count, and they kept counting until Craig hit 40 reps. When Monson slammed done the weights, he made his statement and the crowd saw a show. Big Craig hit 315 for 40 reps. It was almost like the old days at the pit in Venice. His body was awake, his mind was clear, and Craig was back with the weights.

The validation that came with a public show of strength was matched by the respect Craig still received among the circles of strength and from graduates of the Los Angeles gang life.

One night while working at Dublin's, Craig saw that Hulk Hogan was in the club. Craig had mentioned to some of the other bouncers that he used to train with him, so they started to joke with Craig, urging him to go say hello because they figured that Hogan wouldn't remember him. Craig didn't take the bait; he held back and kept his own company, until Hulk saw his old training and drinking partner. With wide smiles, the two lifters embraced warmly and shared tales of the old days on Venice Beach, while Craig's fellow bouncers stared on in wide-eyed awe and admiration for the coworker who had been maintaining his "undercover" status.

On another occasion, rapper Snoop Dogg came into the club. When he saw Big Craig, he did a double take.

"What's your name?" the former Long Beach Crip turned international rap sensation asked Craig.

"I'm Craig Monson."

"Ah, shit! You're the Godfather!"

"The Godfather?"

"Yeah, you started all this shit!"

Not just a lyrical poet of urban life, but also a student of the great street legends, Snoop grew up hearing stories about Craig and his pivotal role in the transformation of gang life across California.

For Craig, this was fulfilling.

You see, in the environment from which Craig came, a lot of people did not have a lot of stuff. What they had was their reputation. This was everything. A strong reputation can provide an individual with a sense of self-worth. And an enduring reputation can provide an individual with a sense of immortality.

After working a number of years at Dublin's, Craig transitioned into private bodyguard work. These days, Craig still calls Los Angeles home. He is still lifting. A regular at Hollywood Gym, Monson keeps chasing the euphoric feeling of "the pump."

In conversations on strength, his name is still spoken and the stories are still told. But, there is an emerging interest in Big Monson. Social media stars, who themselves grew up hearing about Big Craig Monson of the Avenues turned international bodybuilding sensation, have created a platform for a wider audience and a new generation of lifting enthusiasts to hear about Craig.

In a time when most daily activities require minimal brute power, when many look for a quick "hack" for success, and when fame comes to sensationalists, Craig is a throwback. Big Monson is an embodiment of unapologetic, chiseled strength, attained through hard work, and recognized for a lifetime of lifting achievement.

In this way, it is a story of authentic strength.

THE WORKOUT

As a teenager, then behind bars, and finally as a free man, Craig aggressively built his body with a blend of heavy-ass pig iron and wicked volume. This journey was characterized by strength and competing to be the alpha male; Craig used all his vital energy to be the best he could be.

As his competitive bodybuilding journey came to a close, Craig slowly lost his feeling of invincibility and fully realized his mortality. All men go through this wounded stage.

Craig overcame and gained immense wisdom in the process. He is living his best life now and continues his growth holistically with a new depth and richness and lives life to the fullest.

He has become a sort of sage to bodybuilders around the world. Craig has experienced life, has grown through his wounds, and now mentors the younger generation. He realized aging is not something to be despised and that the up-and-coming generation can learn a lot from the old heads. Craig gleefully passes the baton to the next generation.

Craig's Advice

Over time, the body changes. Craig fully acknowledges this, but just because you turn 50, that doesn't mean you have to trade in your barbell for pink panties. He believes the following strategies can help the aging lifter continue to make gains and feel good. This is not just pie-in-the-sky theory; he continued to have a pro bodybuilder physique well into his sixties.

Craig offers the following tips to lifters battling Father Time:

Technique is #1 Start viewing a breakdown in form as a weakness. Push yourself as hard as possible, but never at the expense of technical execution.

Lighter Weights on Isolation Exercises As lifters age, inevitably, there is wear and tear to cartilage surrounding the joints. This means you are more vulnerable to injuries in the elbows, knees, and shoulders. Isolation movements stress a single joint, so keep things like skull crushers to higher reps. Don't worry about breaking personal records; instead, focus on the mind-muscle connection. If you cannot feel a set, kill the set! Avoid things like cheat curls and swinging lateral raises.

Properly Warm Up When in doubt, warm up more! It is way better to be slightly fatigued than to be cold.

Sleep The days of lifting in the day, partying in the night, then repeating are over. You can increase your rate of recovery with more sleep. In a perfect world, you will sleep eight hours per night. Build a sleep ritual. Sleep in a cool, dark room on a comfortable and supportive mattress. Avoid caffeine, alcohol, and intense exercise late in the evening. Turn off electronic devices.

Plan Ahead For training, nutrition, and sleep, failure to plan is planning to fail. Prep your meals, block off time to train, and make sure you are in bed on time—it all starts with a plan.

Be Flexible in the Gym If your program calls for five sets of bench press, but you feel crazy fatigued after two, don't force five. Something still beats nothing; you still get a training stimulus, but you hit the brakes before digging too deep and getting injured.

Check Your Hormones Over time, hormonal levels decrease, but sometimes this decrease expedites and kills any chance of gains and is downright unhealthy. If you are not feeling like your old self, make an appointment with an endocrinologist and see if hormone replacement therapy is an option.

Final Thoughts

As Craig aged, he didn't adopt a gimmicky, silver-sneakers type of training routine. He trained much the same as he did in his bodybuilding days. The biggest difference was the cloak-and-dagger training tips Craig has so graciously shared.

Craig is a bona fide legend keen on helping the next generation of bodybuilders, while helping the current aging generation maintain and even gain into their golden years.

Made in United States
Orlando, FL
21 November 2023

39251067R00059